PARTY GAMES
FOR ALL

EVERYDAY HANDBOOKS

PARTY GAMES
FOR ALL

Bernard S. Mason
Elmer D. Mitchell

BARNES & NOBLE, INC. · NEW YORK

PUBLISHERS · BOOKSELLERS · SINCE 1874

L. C. Catalogue Card Number: 47-4952

TABLE OF CONTENTS

CHAPTER I

THE RECREATIONAL CALENDAR

IN PLANNING recreational programs of a social nature, play leaders and hosts frequently desire to build the program around some particular theme. Of the many possibilities for such themes, the use of holidays and historical events connected with the week or month of the function is a method particularly appealing to many.

With many groups, and in many settings, such a procedure would be unwise and undesirable; in other situations it is admirable. Whether or not the program is centered around the commemoration of any historical event, it is usually desirable to make the decorations and favors seasonal in nature. Even though no particular theme runs through the party, references to appropriate historical events and holidays are frequently desirable in connection with particular games used in the program.

The following calendar of dates of various types may contain suggestions useful to recreational leaders and those who are called upon to plan for parties, dances, dinners, and so forth. Unless otherwise stated, when the name of an individual appears with a certain date, the date is that individual's birthday.

JANUARY

1st	New Year's Day
1st	Paul Revere, 1735
1st	Negro Emancipation, 1863
3rd	Cicero, B. C. 106
6th	Epiphany (Celebrates arrival of the three kings at the crib in Bethlehem)
7th	Gregory XIII (Ugo Buoncompagni) 1502. (Our present calendar is known as the Gregorian Calendar)
11th	Alexander Hamilton, 1757
17th	Benjamin Franklin, 1706
17th	Thrift Week starts about this date each year
18th	Daniel Webster, 1782
19th	Robert E. Lee, 1807
19th	Edgar Allan Poe, 1809
21st	Stonewall Jackson, 1824

1

24th Frederick the Great, 1712
24th Gold discovered in California, 1848
25th Robert Burns, 1759
27th Mozart, 1756
27th William McKinley, 1843
31st Franz Schubert, 1797

FEBRUARY

2nd Groundhog Day
2nd Young Peoples' Society of Christian Endeavor founded, 1881
5th Dwight L. Moody, 1837
7th Charles Dickens, 1812
8th Boy Scouts of America, 1910
8th John Ruskin, 1819
11th Thomas A. Edison, 1847
12th Abraham Lincoln, 1809
12th Charles Darwin, 1809
14th St. Valentine's Day
21st Battle of Verdun, 1916
21st Cardinal John Henry Newman, 1801
22nd George Washington, 1732
22nd Lord Robert Baden-Powell, 1857
22nd James Russell Lowell, 1819
23rd Handel, 1685
26th Buffalo Bill (William Frederick Cody), 1845
27th Henry W. Longfellow, 1807
29th Leap Year
First Monday Arbor Day in Arizona
First Friday Arbor Day in Florida
Lent begins Wednesday, six and one-half weeks before Easter Sunday

MARCH

3rd Alexander Graham Bell, 1847
6th Michelangelo, 1475
7th Luther Burbank, 1849
17th St. Patrick's Day
19th David Livingstone, 1813
21st First Day of Spring
Easter—earliest possible date, March 24; latest possible date, April 25

APRIL

1st All Fool's Day
1st Bismarck, 1815

3rd   First pony express riders started between Sacramento and St. Joseph, Missouri, 1860
3rd   Washington Irving, 1783
3rd   John Burroughs, 1837
6th   R. E. Peary discovered the North Pole, 1909
9th   Lee surrendered to Grant, 1865
10th William Booth (founder of Salvation Army), 1829
13th Thomas Jefferson, 1743
18th Paul Revere's Ride, 1775
19th Patriot's Day—Battle of Lexington and Concord, 1775
22nd Arbor Day in Nebraska
23rd William Shakespeare, 1564
26th Confederate Memorial Day in Alabama, Florida, Georgia, and Mississippi
27th Ulysses S. Grant, 1822
30th Washington inaugurated First President of United States, 1789
Third Tuesday Arbor Day in Montana

MAY

1st   May Day
3rd   Poland, Constitution Day, 1791
4th   John J. Audubon, 1780
5th   Nebori-no-Sekku, Japan, Feast of Flags
6th   Robert E. Peary, 1856
9th   R. E. Byrd flew to North Pole, 1926
9th   Australia, Federation Day
10th Confederate Memorial Day in North Carolina and South Carolina
12th Florence Nightingale, 1820
15th First Air Mail Service, 1918
15th Epworth League, 1889
16th Joan of Arc, 1412
17th Norway, Independence Day
18th World Peace Day
21st Y. W. C. A.—Grace H. Dodge Day
21st Charles A. Lindbergh flew the Atlantic, 1927
21st American Association of the Red Cross founded, 1881
24th Empire Day in the British Empire
24th Queen Victoria, 1819
25th Ralph Waldo Emerson, 1803
30th Memorial Day or Decoration Day
First Friday Arbor Day in Idaho
Second Friday Arbor Day in Rhode Island
Second Sunday Mother's Day
Second Sunday Confederate Day in Tennessee
Ascension Day—40 days after Easter
Pentecost—50 days after Easter

JUNE

3rd	Jefferson Davis, 1808
5th	Denmark, Constitution Day, 1849
10th	China, Dragon Boat Festival
11th	Hawaii—Kamehameha, First King
14th	Flag Day, 1777
14th	Harriet Beecher Stowe, 1811
17th	Battle of Bunker Hill, 1775
18th	Battle of Waterloo, 1815
21st	First Day of Summer. Longest day of year.
21st	Daniel Carter Beard, 1850
24th	Henry Ward Beecher, 1813
25th	Custer's defeat at Big Horn, Montana, by Sitting Bull, 1876
27th	Helen Keller, 1880
28th	John Wesley, 1703
Second Sunday	Children's Day
Third Sunday	Father's Day

JULY

1st	Dominion Day in Canada
1st to 3rd	Battle of Gettysburg, 1863
4th	Independence Day, 1776
4th	Nathaniel Hawthorne, 1804
4th	Giuseppe Garibaldi, 1807
5th	P. T. Barnum, 1810
5th	Venezuela, Independence Day, 1811
6th	John Paul Jones, 1747
9th	Argentina, Independence Day, 1816
12th	Julius Caesar, B. C. 100
12th	Orangemen's Day in Canada (Battle of the Boyne)
14th	France, Bastille Day
15th	Battle of Château-Thierry, 1918
15th	Rembrandt, 1607
21st	Battle of Bull Run, 1861
21st	Belgium, Independence Day, 1831
22nd	Gregor Johann Mendel, 1822
28th	Peru, Independence Day, 1921

AUGUST

6th	Alfred Tennyson, 1809
9th	Izaac Walton, 1593
11th	Fulton's steamboat, 1807
11th	Germany, Constitution Day, 1919
14th	Ernest Thompson Seton, 1860
15th	Sir Walter Scott, 1771

17th   David Crockett, 1786
28th   Goethe, 1749
29th   Oliver Wendell Holmes, 1809

SEPTEMBER

6th   Lafayette Day, Marquis de Lafayette, 1757
7th   Brazil, Independence Day, 1822
13th   John J. Pershing, 1860
14th   Star Spangled Banner written by Francis Scott Key,
        1814
15th   James Fenimore Cooper, 1789
16th   Pilgrims sailed from England, 1620
16th   Mexico, Independence Day, 1821
17th   Constitution Day, 1787
20th   Italy, Unification Day, 1870
22nd   Emancipation Proclamation, 1862
23rd   First Day of Autumn
First Monday Labor Day

OCTOBER

7th   James Whitcomb Riley, 1853
9th   Fire Prevention Day (Chicago Fire—1871)
10th   China, Independence Day, 1911
11th   Sir George Williams, 1821 (Founded Y. M. C. A. in
        1844)
12th   Columbus Day (America discovered, 1492)
15th   Vergil, 70 B. C.
27th   Theodore Roosevelt, 1858
28th   Czechoslovakia, Independence Day
31st   Hallowe'en
31st   Luther nailed his ninety-five theses, 1517

NOVEMBER

1st   All Saints' Day
2nd   Daniel Boone, 1734
——   Election Day (First Tuesday after First Monday)
10th   Martin Luther, 1483
11th   Armistice Day, 1918
11th   Indian Summer begins (St. Martin's Summer in Eng-
        land and France)
13th   Edwin Booth, 1833
13th   Robert Louis Stevenson, 1850
19th   Lincoln's Gettysburg Address, 1863
Last Thursday Thanksgiving Day
        Advent (Church preparation for Christmas). Begins
        four Sundays before Christmas

DECEMBER

6th	Saint Nicholas, patron saint of children
9th	John Milton, 1608
14th	Amundsen reached South Pole, 1911
16th	Beethoven, 1770
16th	Boston Tea Party, 1773
17th	John Greenleaf Whittier, 1807
17th	Wright Brothers' first airplane flight, 1903
21st	First day of winter. Shortest day of year
21st	Mayflower landed at Plymouth
24th	Kit Carson, 1809
25th	Christmas
25th	Washington crossed the Delaware River, 1776
27th	Louis Pasteur, 1822
28th	Woodrow Wilson, 1856
29th	William E. Gladstone, 1809
30th	Rudyard Kipling, 1865
31st	New Year's Eve
First Friday	Arbor Day in Georgia

CHAPTER II

SOCIAL MIXERS

SOCIAL GATHERINGS are usually more or less formal and "stiff" at the start, particularly if there are strangers in the group. The guests are inclined to be reserved, quiet, and on guard. Even if the group is composed of friends who have been together frequently, the party "warms up" slowly and there is an entirely different feeling near the end than at the start.

The business of the host or leader is to get everyone acquainted at once and to establish a feeling of complete rapport as quickly as possible. The sooner everyone is entirely at ease and free to be himself, the greater the possibility of a successful evening. The period of formality is lost time, and a skillful leader or host will end it promptly.

Toward this end mixers are used. Whatever helps to break down formality, introduce strangers, start conversation, and induce laughter, serves the purpose of a mixer. The following are events that help to accomplish these results.

Receiving Line

Parties, Receptions, Social Gatherings　　*Intermediates to Adults*

At those social gatherings where it is desirable to present everyone to everyone else in a somewhat formal way, a receiving line is the most expedient device.

Start the line at a definite place near the entrance, with the hosts, leaders, chaperones, and special guests at the head of the line. Each guest, upon entering, introduces himself to the head of the line and is then introduced by him to the second person, and so on down the line.

Upon reaching the end of the line each person falls in at the end and thus meets all those who arrive later.

Famous Characters Receiving Line

Parties, Social Gatherings　　　　　　*Intermediates to Adults*

This is a humorous adaptation of the Receiving Line, which immediately creates a fun-making situation that carries on throughout the evening. It "breaks the ice" with the first introduction.

Each guest is assigned the name of a Biblical character which is used throughout the introductions instead of his own name. The leader stands at the head of the line with a card on which he has jotted down possible names. No warning is given a guest as he arrives and he is greeted by the leader with the name he is to carry for the evening.

For example, as a new arrival approaches, the leader might say, "Good evening, Moses, I'm delighted to see you. I am St. Peter." Then turning to the next person in line he might say "King Solomon, may I present Moses?"

Instead of using Biblical names, *famous historical characters* may be used, such as Julius Caesar, Nero, Cleopatra, Henry VIII, Rasputin, and so forth.

The names of *moving picture actors and actresses* are particularly appropriate for some groups and occasions.

Mixing Circle

Dances, Parties, Social Gatherings   *Juniors to Adults*

This is one of the best of the more formal methods of mixing. Form two large circles, one inside the other, with the boys forming the outer circle and the girls the inner. At the command "Ladies to the right, gentlemen to the left—forward, march!", the piano or orchestra strikes up and the two circles march. In a moment the music stops, and the two circles face each other. Each person shakes hands with the person in the other circle who is nearest, tells his name, and talks until the music starts again. The stops should be frequent.

It is well for the leader, each time the music stops, to announce subjects for conversation or movements to be made. The following may be used:

1. Girls skip around your partner three times.
2. Tell your partner your name, where you were born, present and future address, who your parents and grandparents were.
3. Tell who your favorite movie actor and actress is, and why.
4. Tell what motion picture of the past year you consider the best, and why.
5. Which is your favorite orchestra?
6. Tell your partner about your views on politics (prohibition, blue laws, woman's ability to drive a car, the season's fashions, jazz, if I were president of the United States).
7. Where do you spend your vacations?
8. Assume a pose of a girl seeing a mouse (Sir Walter Raleigh as Queen Elizabeth approaches, a boy stubbing his toe, a preacher exhorting his flock, and so forth).

Squawker Mixer

Ballroom Dances, Parties, Social   *Intermediates to Adults*
Gatherings

Form a circle around the room with one extra person in the center who acts as starter. The starter has a loud squawker, or some article which, when dropped on the floor, will make sufficient noise for all to hear.

The starter goes up to a person in the line, calls out his own name and asks the other person to do the same. They then shake hands and the starter continues to the right, shaking hands and introducing himself to every second person in the line. The person he has met starts in the opposite direction introducing himself to every second person. Each person as he is met starts in the direction opposite to that from which the person who met him came. The game goes on in this manner until the whole circle is mixed up. The starter gives the signal by using the squawker, and all guests resume their original positions in the circle.

The last person getting back to his or her position must obtain the squawker or other article used for signalling and start the game again. Play quickly for about five minutes.

Lotto Mixer

Parties   *Seniors to Adults*

Prepare beforehand a sheet of paper for each guest, marked out into twenty-five squares, five squares in each row. The squares should be about a half inch in size. Give each guest a paper as he arrives and ask him to introduce himself to twenty-five people and write the name of each in one of the squares. When all have their twenty-five squares filled, assemble the guests, and have each in turn read one name from his sheet. As a name is read, each guest checks the square on his sheet in which that name appears. The first person to have five checks in a row calls out "Lotto!" and wins the prize.

Paper Handshake

Parties, Dances   *Juniors to Adults*

Each member of the reception committee wears a paper bag on his right hand. As a guest arrives a paper bag is put on his hand and he is asked to shake hands with every person present while wearing the bag.

Left Handed Mixer

Parties, Social Gatherings   *Juniors to Adults*

The guests are notified upon entering that all handshaking must be done with the left hand. Give each a large autograph card and announce a prize for the greatest number of autographs secured in twenty minutes. All autographs, however, must be written with the left hand. When refreshment time comes, the left hand must be used.

Odd or Even

Party   *Juniors to Adults*

Each person is given a dozen or so peanuts. The object is to get as many nuts from the others as possible. Don goes up to Dorothy with a number of nuts concealed in his hand, and says "Odd or Even?" Dorothy guesses "Odd," and since there are seven peanuts in Don's hand, she collects the seven peanuts. If the guess had been wrong, Dorothy would have had to turn over to Don the number of nuts he held.

Quarter in the Crowd

Parties, Social Gatherings   *Juniors to Adults*

This is a good mixer which will get everyone shaking hands. The leader or the committee in charge donates a quarter to the cause. This is given to someone in the group. The others do not, of course, know who holds it. The leader announces that the one holding the quarter will give it to the tenth person who shakes hands with him. Everyone at once begins shaking hands. The one who holds the quarter puts it in his pocket, keeps an accurate count, and gives it to the tenth person (or whatever number is announced).

If the group is large, give several dimes to the person, and have him give one to each seventh person who shakes his hand.

MILLIONAIRE FRIENDS.—This is on the order of Quarter in the Crowd. The quarter is given to a couple, one of whom holds it until their identity has been discovered. The couple may separate and join occasionally at will. They give the money prize to the one who first addresses them when they are together with the words, "I am in need of money. Will you lend me a quarter?" In large groups it would be well to have three or four couples each holding a quarter.

The Mysterious Couple

Parties, Social Gatherings   *Juniors to Adults*

This event has the desirable feature of starting conversation immediately and causing everyone to circulate, and that is all that can be asked of a mixer.

Announce that there is a mysterious couple in the crowd whose identity can be discovered only by careful search and inquiry, and that a prize will go to the individual who first makes the identification. The couple need not necessarily be a man and woman, but may be two women or two men. They need not be together all the time but, of course, should be occasionally.

The guests immediately start asking every couple seen together if they are the mysterious couple. When they are discovered they must admit it and record the name of the finder, asking him to keep quiet until the second and third place winners have been determined. Then the guests are assembled and the prizes awarded.

What You're Doing

Parties, Social Gatherings   *Intermediates to Adults*

The leader selects three leaders and coaches them beforehand. One leader moves around among the guests and whispers to each the name of some person with whom he or she is supposed to be. The second leader whispers to each player where he is, and the third what he is doing. The leaders, of course, work independently.

The group is then assembled and each person stands, states his name, tells whom he is with, where he is, and what he is doing. For example, one might say, "My name is Bill Smith. I'm with Winnie West, at Peking, China, washing pajamas."

Get-Acquainted Excursion

Parties, Social Gatherings   *Juniors to Adults*

Arrange chairs to represent a train. There should be two chairs for each seat on each side of the aisle. Have the guests sit in the chairs, a boy and a girl to each seat. There should be a conductor, brakeman, paper boy, and candy and sandwich vender, each playing his characteristic rôle. If care is taken in casting these rôles, much humor will be added.

The conductor calls his stations at frequent intervals. Each time a station is called all the boys get up and move forward one seat. In this way they are placed in situations where conversation is required.

Autograph Cards

In large gatherings where people do not know each other, such as college freshman get-togethers and mixers, give each person a large autograph card as he enters on which he is to secure the signature and address of each person with whom he converses. A small prize may be given late in the evening for the longest list of autographs. Each takes the card home with him.

Meet the Poets

This clever little event leads to much amusement in any group and serves admirably as a get-acquainted mixer.

The leader announces that he is going to give each person a number and then call on each one to stand and recite a little poem containing his name and number. Allow about five minutes for the guests to compose their rhymes.

Examples from a recent party are as follows:

> My number is four
> And my name is Stone.
> I've been here before
> And I'd rather stay home.

> My name is Bill Stokes
> And my number is one.
> I do not mind jokes
> If they lead to fun.

> My number is four
> And my name is Jones.
> My favorite sport
> Is rolling the bones.

> I never was a lucky soul
> Good fortune ne'er was mine,
> For what will rhyme with Davidson
> Or even with number nine?

People of all ages will contribute many clever rhymes.

Yes or No

As each guest enters he is given ten beans or grains of corn. The guests are then told to ask questions of each other, collecting a bean from everyone who answers a question with the words "yes" or "no." A prize is awarded to the one having the largest number of beans when time is called.

Introductions

Parties, Social Gatherings   *Adults*

This mixer is very efficient to familiarize everyone with the names of the others. The guests are all seated. The leader arises and says, "It's a pleasure to meet you all. My name is Stowe." The next person stands and says, "How do you do, Mr. Stowe, my name is Miss Stearns." The third stands and says, "How do you do, Mr. Stowe and Miss Stearns, my name is Mr. Barker." The fourth says, "How do you do, Mr. Stowe, Miss Stearns, and Mr. Barker, my name is Miss Conley." And each person must mention in turn the names of all who have already introduced themselves.

How Is Your Neighbor?

Parties, Social Gatherings   *Juniors to Adults*

The players are seated in a circle with "it" standing in the center. There are just enough chairs for those seated but none for "it." "It" approaches one of the players and asks "Who are your neighbors?" If he cannot name them correctly he must exchange places with "it." If he does name them, "it" asks further, "How is Mr.——," naming one of the player's neighbors. If the reply is "All right," everyone shifts one seat to the right; if he says "All righteous," they shift to the left; if the reply is "Not so good," everyone shifts anywhere he pleases. During the shifting, "it" attempts to get a seat and the person left without a seat becomes "it."

Bumpety-Bump-Bump

Parties, Social Gatherings   *Juniors to Adults*

The players stand or sit in a large circle. Have one player acting as "it" for each ten players in the circle. The "its" are in the center of the circle.

The players are given a moment to learn the names of their neighbors on either side. The "its" run up to anyone in the circle, point to him and say "Right—bumpety, bump, bump," to which the player pointed to must instantly respond with the name of the person on his right. If he fails to respond before "it" says "Bumpety-bump-bump," he changes places with the "it" who pointed to him. "Left—bumpety, bump, bump" may also be used.

Hicky-Hikey-Hokey-Pokey.—This game is the same as Bumpety-Bump-Bump except that the phrase is "Right (or left)—hicky-hikey-hokey-pokey."

LEMON, LEMON.—This is the same as the above except that the phrase is "Right (or left), lemon, lemon, one, two, three, four, five, six, seven."

TURKEY, TURKEY.—This is a variation of the above suitable for Thanksgiving. The phrase is "Right (or left), turkey, turkey, turkey."

ZIP AND ZAP.—The player in the center points to a player and says, "Zip" and counts to five. The player must give the name of his right-hand neighbor before the count is up. If "Zap" is said, the name of the left-hand neighbor must be said.

Farmer Jones' Hen

Party   *Juniors to Adults*

Seat the players in a circle. One player (Joe) starts by saying, "Farmer Jones has a fine red hen." Betty, sitting next to him, asks "Does she cackle?" To which Joe answers, "Yes, she cackles." Betty then turns to the third player (Jim) and the following conversation ensues:

Betty: Farmer Jones has a fine red hen.
Jim: Does she cackle?
Betty to Joe: Does she cackle?
Joe to Betty: Yes, she cackles.
Betty to Jim: Yes, Joe says she cackles.

Thus the game continues, the question being referred back around the circle to the first player in each case, and the names of the preceding players being repeated.

After several have participated, the answer to the question might sound like this: "Yes, Jack says that Sue says that Al says that Peggy says that Jim says that Betty says that Joe says she cackles."

This event has the desirable quality of causing all the names to be repeated, thus familiarizing everyone with everybody else's name.

The game is also good fun if played without the repetition of the names.

DO YOU WANT TO BUY A WHISTLE.—The first player says to the second, "Do you want to buy a whistle?" The second asks, "Does it whistle?" "Yes, it whistles." In other respects, the game is played like the above.

MR. PENNER'S DUCK.—The first player says, "Do you want to buy a duck?" The second says, "Does she quack?" "Yes, she quacks." Otherwise, proceed as above.

Ha, Ha, Ha

Parties   *Intermediates to Adults*

The players are seated in a circle. The first player says "Ha," the second in turn says "Ha, Ha," the third "Ha, Ha, Ha" and so on around the circle, each adding one more "Ha." The "Ha's" must be said without laughing. This proves to be difficult and the entire circle is soon laughing. Those laughing while uttering their "Ha, Ha's" are eliminated. The one staying in the longest wins.

The Blind Guest

Parties   *Intermediates to Adults*

Blindfold a player who is clever at repartee. He moves about among the guests as they are scattered about the room, shakes hands with all whom he can find, engages in conversation with each, and tells each what he thinks of him or her.

Famous Characters

Parties, Social Gatherings   *Juniors to Adults*

Prepare beforehand slips on which are written the names of famous people, both present day and historical. As each guest enters pin a slip on his back without his knowing what it says. The guests observe each other's slips and then converse with one another as though they were talking with the person named on the slip. As this goes on each tries to guess who he is supposed to be. The remarks should not be so leading as to give away the identity too soon. Much interesting and amusing conversation will ensue.

ADVERTISERS.—Pin an advertisement on the back of each guest as he enters. They read each other's advertisements and make comments to them about their products. From the comments each attempts to guess the product he advertises.

The Chief's Orders

Parties, Social Gatherings   *Intermediates to Adults*

As the guests enter give each lady an odd-numbered card and each man an even-numbered card. Each card reads: "The following are the Chief's orders—be sure to carry them out." The following are suggested orders; similar ones may be made up to suit the nature of the program and the interests of the group:

1. You are the official introducer. Find Number 2 and introduce him to Number 12; Number 4 to Number 10; Number 6 to Number 8.
2. Same as the above with a boy introducing the girls.
3. Find Number 16 and ask him to help you ask each boy who his

favorite movie actress is. Later you will be asked to announce your results.

4. Find Number 11 and ask her to help you ask each girl who her favorite movie actor is. Later you will be asked to announce your results.

5. Find Number 14 and ask him to help you find out what each person's favorite radio program is. Later you will be asked to announce your results.

6. Find Number 17 and together list the politics of everyone present.

7. Find Number 12 and together ask each person what he or she considers the best movie of the past year. Later your results will be announced.

8. List all the blond-haired girls.
9. List all the blue-eyed men.
10. List all the brunettes.
11. List all the brown-eyed men.

Word Making Mixer

Parties, Social Gatherings   *Juniors to Adults*

Give each person a lapel card with a large letter on it. There should be a generous supply of the more common letters, particularly the vowels, and few of the rare letters. The object is to form words of ten letters. Select a number of leaders to take the initiative. If there are fifty people present, five leaders would be needed.

At the signal the leader secures two or three companions who have letters he thinks he may need. They select the word and start the search for the necessary letters. They will have to move swiftly for the desired letters will soon be picked up.

Each group is called upon to line up and display their word. After each has been on display, the leader may announce that each group will be given three minutes to find another word that can be spelled with the letters they have.

Trading Proverbs

Parties, Social Gatherings   *Intermediates to Adults*

Write proverbs on slips of paper and then cut each into three or four pieces. Pin the pieces on the walls in plain sight.

At the signal the players gather as many slips as they can. Then by trading their slips they try to put together complete proverbs. The one completing the largest number wins. Assemble the guests and have the winner read his proverbs.

A list of over a hundred proverbs that may be used will be found under Split Proverbs (page 30).

First Impressions

Parties   *Intermediates to Adults*

Sheets of paper of three or four different colors are needed, an equal number of each color. Pin a sheet on the back of each guest as he arrives, distributing the colors evenly, and give each a pencil.

All those wearing the same color assemble in a separate corner of the room. The guests then mingle and introduce themselves to each other. After each introduction, each asks the other to write on the paper on his back the first impression of him that came to the other's mind after the introduction. After a few minutes they are instructed to remove the sheets and read the impressions.

Musical Mixer

Parties, Social Gatherings   *Juniors to Adults*

Give each guest as he enters a slip containing the name of a popular song. The guests immediately search for others holding the name of the same song. When the groups are together give them a few moments to converse and get acquainted and then call on each group to sing their song.

Laughing Handkerchief

Parties, Social Gatherings   *Juniors to Adults*

Any device which causes people to laugh serves admirably as a mixer. The laughing in this stunt may be artificial at the start, but it soon becomes spontaneous and natural.

The leader stands where all can see him. He tosses a handkerchief in the air and while it is in the air everyone laughs, but when it touches the floor all must have stopped laughing and assumed a long face. Those who laugh when the handkerchief is not in the air are eliminated and go to one side where they may assist in attempting to make those who are still competing laugh. Likewise those who do not laugh when the handkerchief is in the air are eliminated.

The leader will need an assistant to stand by him and help him pick out those who laugh or not in violation of the rules. The height to which the handkerchief is thrown should be varied so that the players are confused as to the length of the laughing spell. Humorous remarks by the leader between throws makes the long face difficult to maintain.

This contest calls for much self-control, and it will not be long before everyone is eliminated. The last to laugh wins the title of the champion grouch.

Smile

The guests are divided into two teams and line up facing each other about ten feet apart. One team is named "heads" and the other team "tails." The leader tosses a coin and calls out the side that turns up. If it comes up heads, the heads laugh and smile while the tails must keep a straight and sober face. The heads of course attempt to make the tails laugh. All who laugh must join the other team. The coin is then tossed again.

Crossed Wires

The leader instructs all as follows: "With your right hand grab your left ear. Now, with your left hand grab your nose." When each has hold of his ear and nose, the leader calls "Change." The difficulty encountered in reversing the hands is always amusing. Such stunts start laughter and serve to break the formality.

Pat and Rub

This is on the order of Crossed Wires. The leader instructs all to rub their stomachs with their right hands and pat the top of their heads with the left. When he calls "Change" they attempt to pat their stomachs and rub their heads.

After this has been figured out, the leader may ask the players to start as before and then reverse the position of their hands, rubbing their stomachs with their left hands and patting their heads with their right hands.

John Brown's Baby

The leader asks the group to rise to sing a song about John Brown's Baby who is afflicted with a cold on his chest. The tune is that of John Brown's Body.

Together they sing the first verse:

> John Brown's baby had a cold upon his chest,
> John Brown's baby had a cold upon his chest,
> John Brown's baby had a cold upon his chest,
> So they rubbed it with camphorated oil!

The second verse is the same, except that the word "baby" is not sung. Instead, a sign for the word "baby" must be used. This sign is the right hand placed on the left elbow and the left arm swung to and fro as if rocking a baby.

In the third verse the word "cold" is not sung. Instead a cough is given. In the fourth verse "chest" is not sung, and the chest is tapped with the open hand instead. "Rub" is omitted from the next verse, the rubbing motion being made on the chest. In the following verse "camphorated oil" is left out and the motion substituted is the holding of the nose to indicate the odor. By this time the only words left to be sung are "John Brown's . . . had a . . .," and so forth. Whoever speaks a word when a gesture should be given must drop out of the song or be seated.

Community Sneeze

Parties, Social Gatherings   *Juniors to Adults*

While seated, the group is roughly divided into three sections. The leader then asks the first section to say together "Hish" two or three times for practice, the second section "Hash," and the third section "Hosh." He then asks the first section to add "ee," that is, "hishee," the second section "hashee," and the third section "hoshee." The leader then tells the group all to say their word in unison at his signal. The ensuing sound is like an enormous sneeze.

CHAPTER III

SOCIAL DANCING AIDS

A T SOME stages of growth a full evening of social dancing without anything else will prove interesting. The dancing carries sufficient appeal in itself to insure the success of the occasion. With most ages and on most occasions, however, the insertion of dancing games and contests, mixers, and eliminations, is desirable and adds greatly to the enjoyment of the evening.

The use of these events is a distinct aid to sociability. They help the individuals to become acquainted more easily, they lead to conversation, they keep the group moving and overcome self-consciousness, they break up fixed cliques, and in general bring joy in creating a rollicking care-free situation so essential to the success of any social event.

The aids to social dancing fall under the following heads: (1) the grand march, (2) methods of pairing off and changing partners, (3) methods of cutting in or "robbing," (4) elimination dances, and (5) miscellaneous dancing aids.

Dance Problems.—The leader or committee in charge of the dance has a much greater responsibility than the provision of an orchestra and a place with adequate floor space and seating arrangements. An understanding of the human element in the dance is much more important than the mechanical arrangements.

The reticent girl, and particularly the bashful boy, are distinct problems. The confident, aggressive boy, who is attractive and a good dancer, can well take care of himself. He will not want for dancing partners, nor hesitate to secure them in robber dances. Such is not the case with the sensitive and bashful, however, who suffer not only because of lack of partners but because of a consciousness of their bashfulness and lack of social success. The problem centers in seeing that these individuals do more than spend an evening of looking on from the edges. The events described in this chapter are designed to that end. The mere use of these activities, however, may not solve the problem—the leader should circulate constantly and suggest, introduce, and encourage.

Good dancers of both sexes who are lacking in tolerance toward poorer dancers, and inclined to be selfish, are no less a problem.

Their ability in dancing makes them much sought after, and every effort should be made to cause them to circulate. The adolescent dancer who "is not exchanging tonight" not only makes himself unpopular, but militates against the success of the dance as a whole. Dancers of this type do not take kindly to the mixers and pairing-off devices, in that they want to dance with a select few. An admired leader can do much with these types by personal suggestion, causing them to see that they are rude and selfish and are publishing their lack of tolerance and sociability.

Dancers of the type described above are largely the cause of cliques in the dance. There should be ample time for everyone to dance with those with whom he particularly desires to; but in order to produce a social dance instead of one of individual couples and cliques, a few of the mixing dances should be utilized.

The fear of "getting stuck" for the evening, or a considerable portion of it, with an uninteresting person is one of the primary reasons why dancers are reluctant to circulate more freely. Since proper dance etiquette requires that he stay with the girl until someone else asks her to dance, the boy is exceedingly hesitant about asking a girl for a dance when he does not particularly care for her, and is afraid no one else will take her off his hands. This is a perfectly legitimate reason and the dancers cannot be blamed for their hesitancy in such a situation. An occasional mixing circle or the use of one of the devices for changing partners prevents this, and if the dancers know that such dances are in the offing they will feel more free to distribute their dances.

Suggestions on Dance Leadership.—No two dances present exactly the same problems, and consequently it is unwise to plan a program with a view to following it rigidly. The leaders should prepare a list of a number of pairing-off dances, robber dances, and eliminations, and secure the equipment for them, and *then use them only as the dance seems to require them*. Few or all of them may be used as conditions demand. It may be that none of them will be needed.

The leader should move about among the dancers and be alert constantly to their needs. The various aids to dancing in this chapter should be regarded as means to an end rather than ends in themselves. Too many novelties and pairing-off devices are annoying; yet not to use them when occasion demands may permit situations to exist which are equally annoying to many. As a rule these devices are particularly appropriate and necessary for young dancers and those who have recently started to dance, and again for middle-aged dancers and married couples. There is a period in between these two ages when dancing aids are not so necessary nor are they usually welcomed. In this period, for the most part, the dancers are aggressive in securing partners, and through experience in dances are well able to care for themselves. To them, the appeal of the music and the dance is sufficient in itself. This is not always the case with the younger and older dancers.

The master of ceremonies should be pleasing in personality, neat in appearance, and possessed of social graces. His voice should be strong, clear, and pleasing. He should possess a sense of humor, be cheerful always, and never overbearing.

In order to attract attention, he should speak quickly when the music stops, and then wait for quiet and not attempt to shout down the noise. A committee of a few dancers in the group who know the scheduled event can aid him greatly in producing quiet and starting the event.

The master of ceremonies should know very definitely just what he wants the group to do, announce the instructions clearly with the fewest possible words, and demonstrate from the floor if need be. The schooled leaders in the group immediately start it and the rest follow.

Do not continue the novelty dances too long. The time to stop any play activity is when the enjoyment is at its height. To allow interest to wane leaves a bad taste in the mouth.

GRAND MARCH

The Grand March is a traditional device for the opening of a dance of the ballroom type. When properly handled it is a beautiful and colorful spectacle.

The music should be in slow march time. The following figures may be used in the Grand March. They need not all be included, of course—the leader may select from them and compose a routine that is as short or long, simple or complex, as he may desire.

Grand March Figures

1. Have the boys line up in file on one side of the room and the girls on the other. The leader of each line leads his or her line to the rear of the room, meets the other line, and the guests march down the center in a column of two's.

2. Upon reaching the front of the room, the first couple goes to the right, the second to the left, the third to the right, and so forth. Couples meet at the back of the room and come up in a column of four's.

3. The three at the right turn right, and the one on the left turns left; when they meet at the back of the room they come up center

in four's; on reaching the front the three on the left turn left, and the one on the right turns right, meet at the back, and come up the center in four's.

4. The four's divide into two's, going right and left, and when the lines meet at the rear of the room, the couples in the line on the director's left all form arches by holding their inside hands high, while the other line marches under, both lines marching straight ahead. The lines continue around the sides of the hall and when they meet at the front of the room, the other line of couples forms the arches while the former arches pass under.

5. When the lines meet at the rear of the room, the first couple on the director's left turns down the center, forms an arch, and the first couple on the right goes under it. They then reverse their positions, and the other couple forms the arch and the former arch goes under it. They thus alternate, moving over and under as they go down the center of the floor, all couples doing the same.

6. When the lines reach the front of the room, the couples march right and left as in Number 2. When they meet at the rear of the room, the first couple on the director's left goes straight ahead, forms an arch, and the first couple on the director's right goes under the arch. The couple that formed the arch, keeping hands joined, goes under an arch formed by the second couple in the opposite line, then forms an arch for the third couple to go under, and so on. All players in both lines, going in opposite directions, do the same. Thus all couples are going under arches and forming arches alternately. They continue around the edge of the room, and when the two lines meet again at the front of the room, the same weaving figure is repeated and the lines continue going around the sides of the room until they meet at the rear.

7. When the two lines meet at the rear of the room, the first couple of each line join hands and the four skip around in a circle for seven counts. On the eight count, the couple on the left goes under an arch formed by the right-side couple, each couple going forward in eight counts to meet the next couple of the opposite line and repeat. This is continued through the line until the leading couples meet again.

8. When the two lines meet at the rear of the room, they come up the center of the floor in four's, and on reaching the front, the first four turn right, the second four turn left; when the two columns of four's meet at the rear of the room, they come up the center in eight's, halting at the front of the room. Eight's join hands and the leader joins on the right of the front line. He leads the front line into a winding formation to the right so that

attachment can be made with the second line (the last one of the first line joining hands with the one on the right of the second line). When all the group is in line, players form a circle.

9. Partners face and grand right and left (see p. 37) around the circle to own partner. The leader winds up the circle by leading the players inside the outside circle. When the players are wound up, the leader unwinds by turning outside, and walking with back to the players who are still winding up.

10. Two circles are formed, girls inside, boys outside. The boys make arches by lifting joined hands. The girls join hands and follow the leader in and out of the arches. The boys take girls on their right and march around the circle in two's, coming up the center of the room in four's.

11. The two inside lines form arches while the outside lines march forward, meet a new partner at the front of the room, turn and march back under arches.

METHODS OF PAIRING OFF AND CHANGING PARTNERS

In dancing groups and at parties it is usually desirable to use devices which will mix the two sexes by chance and prevent couples from staying together throughout the entire evening. Otherwise certain girls will be neglected and shy boys will not have the good time that otherwise might be possible. The following devices may be used as methods of pairing off at the start of the dance or party, and as means of mixing the group during the course of the evening.

Simple Grand March

Ballroom Dances, Parties   *Juniors to Adults*

The simplest method of pairing off is to conduct a simplified grand march. Ask the boys to line up outside one door on one side of the room and the girls at another. The two lines march around, meet, and line up side by side. The players standing together are partners for the next dance.

Matching Numbers

Ballroom Dances, Parties   *Juniors to Adults*

Prepare duplicate slips of paper each containing a number. Pass out one set to the girls and the other to the boys. Each then circulates and tries to find the member of the opposite sex who has the same number. These two are partners.

VARIATION.—The boys holding odd numbers may dance with any girl holding an odd number. That is, a boy holding Number 1 may dance with the girl holding Number 1, 3, 5, 7 and so forth.

VARIATION.—The boys holding odd numbers may dance with any girl holding an even number, and vice versa.

VARIATION.—Groups of numbers dance together. For example, the boys holding numbers between 1 and 5 may dance with any girl holding a number between 1 and 5.

Name Dance

Ballroom Dances, Parties   *Juniors to Adults*

Place slips containing the boys' names in a box and have the girls draw for their dancing partners.

Famous Character Dance

Ballroom Dances, Parties   *Juniors to Adults*

This is one of the best of the methods of pairing off and is a great fun-maker. Prepare slips for the girls giving each a name of some famous woman of history and telling her to dance with some famous man of history. Prepare similar slips for the boys. For example: a girl's slip might read "You are Cleopatra. Dance with Julius Caesar," or "You are Queen Elizabeth. Dance with Nero." The corresponding boys' slips would read, "You are Julius Caesar. Dance with Cleopatra" and "You are Nero. Dance with Queen Elizabeth."

The slips are distributed and all search for their dancing partners. The following types of characters may be used:

Moving picture actors and actresses.
Famous poets, authors.
Famous characters of fiction.
Pioneers, Indians, cowboys, western badmen.
Famous artists.
Famous musicians and composers.

Matching Flowers

Ballroom Dances, Parties   *Juniors to Adults*

Give each boy and each girl a flower. There should be as many different kinds of flowers as possible. Each boy finds the girl whose flower matches his. If it is necessary to use more than one of each kind of flower, it makes little difference. Some flowers may be marked with colored ribbon if necessary to make enough different kinds.

MATCHING HATS.—Give out paper hats to all. Each boy dances with the girl whose hat exactly matches his.

Matching Playing Cards

Ballroom Dances, Parties   *Juniors to Adults*

Give each girl a playing card from one deck of cards and each boy a card from another deck. They find their dancing partners by matching the cards.

If there are not enough dancers to use two packs, use only one and give the red cards to the girls and the black cards to the boys. Announce that the spades dance with the corresponding hearts, and the clubs with the corresponding diamonds.

Matching Circles

Ballroom Dances   *Juniors to Adults*

Cut out cardboard into perfect circles about four inches in diameter, one circle for each couple expected. Then cut each circle in two, placing one part in the girls' pile and one part in the boys' pile. Each circle should be cut at a different angle. Give each girl one of the cardboard pieces and each boy one. Each boy searches until he finds a girl whose cardboard matches his and makes a perfect circle. These two are partners.

VARIATION.—Instead of cutting up circles, cut Valentines, cardboard Christmas bells, Christmas trees, shamrocks, hatchets, Easter Eggs, or any symbol characteristic of the season of the dance.

Matching Advertisements

Parties, Ballroom Dances   *Juniors to Adults*

Cut advertisements from newspapers and magazines and cut each advertisement in half. As the guests enter give each one half of an advertisement. One half of each is given to a boy and the other half to a girl. Each guest finds the person who has the other half of his advertisement. These two are partners for the first dance.

Lollypop Dance

Ballroom Dances, Parties   *Juniors to Adults*

Write the name of a girl on each lollypop given to the boys, and the name of a boy on each given to the girls. Each boy finds the girl whose name appears on his lollypop and dances with her. When the signal is given the music stops and the couples separate, each girl finding the boy whose name appears on her lollypop.

Lollypop Doll Dance

Ballroom Dances, Parties   *Juniors to Adults*

Paint faces on enough lollypops so that there will be one for each guest expected. Each face should be duplicated on another lollypop, thus making a pair with duplicate faces. The faces on each pair should differ in detail from those on all the other lollypops. One set is given to the boys and the duplicates to the girls. They hunt until they match their lollypops exactly and thus find their dancing partners.

States and Capitals

Parties, Ballroom Dances   *Intermediates and Adults*

Give each boy a slip containing the name of a state and each girl a slip containing the name of the capital of a state. They circulate until they find their partners.

VARIATION.—Pin on each girl a paper containing the outline of a state. Give the boys slips containing the names of capitals of states. Each boy finds the girl possessing the outline of the state whose capital he holds.

Description Dance

Ballroom Dances, Parties   *Intermediates to Adults*

Each girl is given a card and pencil. Each writes a description of herself and her dress. The cards are thrown in a hat. Each boy draws one and finds the girl described for his partner.

Dance of the Professions

Ballroom Dances, Parties   *Adults*

Each man is given a card on which he writes his profession and any remarks about it he may choose. The cards are thrown in a hat and each lady picks one. She finds the man described, and dances with him.

Clapping In and Clapping Out

Ballroom Dances, Parties   *Juniors, Intermediates*

Assemble the boys in one room and the girls in another. Arrange a circle of chairs in the girls' room, and have each girl stand behind a chair. Have each girl draw a number. In the meantime, each boy in the boys' room has drawn a number.

Call in a boy and announce his number. As he enters, the girls all clap. He sits down in one of the chairs, and if the girl behind the chair does not have the same number as he, he is clapped out of the chair. Thus he moves from chair to chair until the clapping ceases, which indicates that he has found the right seat. Then another boy is called in and his number announced, and so on. Continue until all the boys have found their partners.

Slipper Dance

Ballroom Dances, Parties   *Juniors to Adults*

This dance is acceptable for young dancers. The boys line up at one end of the floor and the girls assemble at the other. Each girl removes one shoe. These are placed in a basket and the basket covered. The basket is passed to the boys who reach under the cover and pull out a shoe. They then go to the girls and match the shoe. Each dances with the owner of the shoe.

VARIATION.—Place the shoes in a pile in the center of the floor. At the signal the boys rush for the shoes and select one.

Balloon Grab

Ballroom Dances, Parties   *Juniors to Adults*

Each girl is given a toy balloon, shipping tag, string, and pencil. Each blows up her balloon, attaches the tag to it, and writes her name on the tag.

The girls form a circle and the boys form a larger circle outside. The girls march to the left; the boys to the right. When the music stops, the girls toss their balloons in the air and bat them into the center of the circle. The boys dash for them and dance with the girl whose name appears on the tag.

The Balloon Bursting Dance (page 43) makes an excellent conclusion for this dance.

Choose Your Hand

Ballroom Dances, Parties   *Juniors to Adults*

Have all the girls go on the stage or behind a curtain. They all thrust a hand under the curtain. The boys, standing on the other side of the curtain, each select a hand and dance with the girl whose hand was chosen.

Having selected a hand, the boy stands by to claim the girl—the girls do not leave their positions until the signal is given after all hands are chosen.

CHOOSE YOUR FOOT.—This variation is acceptable for young children. It is the same as the above except that the girls all remove one shoe and thrust a foot under a curtain or sheet.

While this mixer may be used without having the girls remove their shoes, it is less satisfactory if conducted in this way, in that the boys may recognize some of the shoes and thus know who the wearers are.

Silhouettes

Ballroom Dances, Parties   *Juniors to Seniors*

This is good at a small dance or party where all know each other. Each boy in turn stands behind a sheet with a light behind him casting his profile on the sheet. The girls attempt to guess the boy. The girl that guesses correctly has him as a partner.

Fish Pond Dance

Ballroom Dances, Parties   *Juniors to Adults*

The girls gather behind a curtain. Each is given a colored ribbon which she throws over the top of the curtain. Each boy selects a ribbon and dances with the girl at the other end.

Affinities

Ballroom Dances, Parties   *Intermediates and Adults*

Write a large number of affinities on slips of paper and cut each in half. "Bread and butter" is an example. "Bread and" would appear on one half and "butter" on the other. Give the first parts to the boys and the last parts to the girls. In this way they find their partners.

Suggested affinities are as follows:

Bread and butter	Shoes and stockings
Salt and pepper	Scotch and soda
Knife and fork	Liver and bacon
Potatoes and meat	Bat and ball
Ham and eggs	Hit and run
Pork and beans	Mother and father
Ice cream and cake	Dog and cat
Pen and ink	Hammer and nail
Paper and pencil	Nut and bolt
Day and night	Gas and oil
Light and dark	Cap and gown
Fair and warmer	Sword and shield
Thunder and lightning	Stocks and bonds
Cup and saucer	Army and navy
Bow and arrow	Stars and stripes
Horse and wagon	Crackers and cheese
House and lot	Lock and key
Coat and hat	Cream and sugar
Collar and tie	Brother and sister

Soap and water	David and Goliath
Comb and brush	Jonah and the whale
Macaroni and cheese	Pat and Mike
Mutt and Jeff	Rod and reel
Anthony and Cleopatra	Fish and chips
Jack and Jill	Saddle and bridle
Adam and Eve	Bag and baggage
Cain and Abel	Needle and thread

Split Proverbs

Ballroom Dances, Parties   *Intermediates and Adults*

Write out proverbs on slips of paper and cut each slip in half. There must be as many cut slips as there are guests expected. Give one half of a proverb to a boy and the other half to a girl. They locate partners by finding the person who has the other half of the proverb. For example, the boy's slip might read "is not gold" and the girl's "all that glitters."

The following are a few proverbs that may be used:

"All that glitters is not gold."
"A stitch in time saves nine."
"A fool and his money are soon parted."
"Every cloud has a silver lining."
"It never rains but it pours."
"Make hay while the sun shines."
"A watched pot never boils."
"A barking dog never bites."
"Never look a gift horse in the mouth."
"A rolling stone gathers no moss."
"Better late than never."
"Birds of a feather flock together."
"A bird in the hand is worth two in the bush."
"Never put off 'till tomorrow what can be done today."
"It's a long lane that has no turning."
"A place for everything and everything in its place."
"Lie down with the dogs, get up with the fleas."
"It's better to have loved and lost, than never to have loved at all."
"Drunken days all have their tomorrows."
"What's good for the goose is good for the gander."
"He laughs best who laughs last."
"There are two sides to every question."
"Out of sight, out of mind."
"As you make your bed, so you must lie in it."
"Too many cooks spoil the broth."
"Rome wasn't built in a day."
"Where there's a will, there's a way."
"You cannot have your cake and eat it too."

"Absence makes the heart grow fonder."

"The early bird catches the worm."

"Everything comes to him who waits."

"Laugh and the world laughs with you; weep and you weep alone."

"Idleness is the mother of evil."

"An empty barrel makes the most noise."

"All's well that ends well."

"A new broom sweeps clean."

"When in Rome, do as the Romans do."

"It's an ill wind that blows nobody good."

"It takes a thief to catch a thief."

"God helps those who help themselves."

"The pot calls the kettle black."

"It's the shovel that laughs at the poker."

"People in glass houses shouldn't throw stones."

"Silence gives consent."

"Well done or not at all."

"A person is known by the company he keeps."

"A word to the wise is sufficient."

"Forewarned is forearmed."

"One good turn deserves another."

"In the kingdom of the blind, the one-eyed are kings."

"All good things must come to an end."

"Everyone knows best where his shoe pinches him."

"Well done is better than well said."

"Contentment is better than riches."

"Health is better than wealth."

"A friend in need is a friend indeed."

"Faint heart never won fair lady."

"To the victor belong the spoils."

"All's fair in love and war."

"The proof of the pudding is in the eating."

"Who counts without his host counts twice."

"One cannot please all the world and his wife."

"He who dances pays the fiddler."

"He who smashes the window pays the glazier."

"Evil to him who evil thinks."

"No pay, no piper."

"Two wrongs do not make a right."

"The pen is mightier than the sword."

"Brevity is the soul of wit."

"Curiosity killed the cat."

"Necessity is the mother of invention."

"Variety is the spice of life."

"He who excuses himself accuses himself."

"It takes two to make a quarrel."

"When a man is wrapped up in himself, the package is small."

"Keep your eyes wide open before marriage, half shut afterwards."

"Speech is silver, silence is golden."

"Take care of the pennies, the dollars will take care of themselves."
"Who steals my purse steals trash."
"There's many a slip 'twixt the cup and the lip."
"Early to bed and early to rise makes a man healthy, wealthy, and wise."
"Discretion is the better part of valor."
"Nothing ventured, nothing gained."
"Handsome is as handsome does."
"They can because they think they can."
"A penny saved is a penny earned."
"Wasteful waste makes woeful want."
"Honesty is the best policy."
"Strike while the iron is hot."
"A bad penny always comes back."
"Enough is as good as a feast."
"You may lead a horse to water, but you can't make him drink."
"Marry in haste, repent at leisure."
"Beggars should not be choosers."
"Like father, like son."
"Once does not make a habit."
"Sorrow treads upon the heels of mirth."
"Hitch your wagon to a star."
"A cloudy morning often changes to a fine day."
"Behind bad luck comes good luck."
"To see an old friend is as agreeable as a good meal."

Old Sayings

Ballroom Dances, Parties   *Intermediates to Adults*

Write old and well-known phrases on slips of paper and cut the slips in half. For example, take the phrase "Strong as an ox." It would be cut in two so that one slip reads "Strong as an" and the other "ox." Give the first parts to the boys and the last parts to the girls. They find the person who has the other half of the saying.

Suggested sayings are as follows:

Strong as an ox	Sour as a lemon
Fat as a pig	White as snow
Hard as a rock	Green as grass
Clear as crystal	Yellow as gold
Thin as a rail	Neat as a pin
Cold as ice	Cross as two sticks
Dead as a doornail	Brave as a lion
Light as a feather	Slow as molasses in January
Sly as a fox	Dry as a bone
Pretty as a picture	Sweet as honey
Black as coal	Hot as fire
Sharp as a razor	Huge as an elephant

Bitter as gall
Heavy as lead
Soft as velvet
Tough as shoe leather
Deep as the ocean
Spry as a spring chicken
Funny as a monkey
Tall as a giraffe
Slippery as an eel
Still as a mouse
Swift as a hare
Bright as the sun
Tight as a drum
Quick as lightning
Poor as a church mouse
Mad as a March hare
Fair as a flower

Ugly as sin
Flat as a pancake
Red as a beet
Crazy as a loon
Brown as a nut
Blind as a bat
Mean as a miser
Full as a tick
Plump as a partridge
Clean as a whistle
Hard as flint
Fine as a fiddle
Stiff as a poker
Calm as a clock
Busy as a bee
Pure as a lily
Proud as a peacock

Matching Poetry

Ballroom Dances, Parties   *Intermediates to Adults*

Select well-known poems, jingles, or limericks and write one or two lines on a slip of paper and the next line or two on another slip. The boys are given one half and the girls the other. Each hunts until he finds the lines that go with those he has.

For example, one slip might read:

> "Under the spreading chestnut tree
> the village smithy stands."

The mate to it would then read:

> "The smith a mighty man is he,
> With large and sinewy hands."

Doubling the Dancers

Ballroom Dances   *Juniors to Adults*

Have the entire group form in a large circle. Select one couple to start dancing in the center. When the music stops the two separate and each selects a new partner and begins dancing again. There are now two couples dancing. Continue until all are selected. The number of dancers doubles each time the music stops.

Balloon Mixer

Ballroom Dances, Parties   *Juniors to Adults*

Write the name of each girl on a slip, roll it and insert it inside a toy balloon. Inflate the balloons and place them inside a large scarf or sheet. Suspend the scarf from the ceiling with a rope attached which is tied to the scarf with a bowknot. At the signal release the balloons by pulling the rope. The boys scramble for them, burst them, and each dances with the girl whose name appears on his slip.

Instead of suspending the balloons from the ceiling, you may hold them in a sheet or scarf and throw them into the center of the floor.

Pantomime Partners

Ballroom Dances, Parties   *Juniors to Adults*

Duplicate slips containing characters which can be easily imitated should be prepared in advance. Assemble the girls at one end of the room and the boys at the other. Pass out one set of slips to the boys and another to the girls. Bring each group up near the center of the floor, and instruct each to impersonate in pantomime the character given him. As soon as a player sees one of the opposite sex impersonating the same character, he or she goes to that person and they are partners.

The following make good characters:

Orchestra director	Piano player
Trombone player	Auctioneer
Golf player	Traffic cop
Tennis player	Truck driver
Baseball pitcher	Ballet dancer
Baseball batter	Father tending baby
Statue of Liberty	Stargazer
Soap-box orator	Table waiter
Ditch digger	Log chopper
Shoe shiner	Toe dancer
Pawn broker	Bullfighter
Indian dancer	Parson
Archer	Skater

Humming Tunes

Ballroom Dances, Parties   *Juniors to Adults*

This is a novel and interesting method of pairing off. Prepare duplicate slips containing the names of tunes which are apt to be familiar to all. One set is handed out to the men and the other to the girls. Instruct the players that positively no words are to be spoken, but each must locate his or her partner by humming the tune from one to another until he finds someone humming the same tune.

Trinket Dance

Ballroom Dances, Parties *Juniors to Adults*

Collect from each girl a trinket, such as a bracelet, flower, or handkerchief. Each boy selects one, finds the owner, and dances with her.

This can be reversed, of course, with the trinkets gathered from the boys, and the girls each selecting one.

Labeled Refreshment Boxes

Ballroom Dances, Parties *Juniors to Adults*

Place the refreshments in lunch boxes and write a girl's name on each box. When the time comes for refreshments each boy is handed a box and eats the lunch with the girl whose name appears on the box.

If the refreshments are to be something like cookies or wafers, ice cream, and punch, each girl may be asked to bring a box containing a dozen or two of cookies or wafers. She writes her name on the box and turns it in upon arrival.

Autograph Program Cards

Ballroom Dances, Parties *Juniors to Adults*

Give each man a card and pencil. Without telling them the purpose, have the men secure as many autographs of girls as possible. This serves as a mixer.

Later when the first event starts, the first name on his card is his partner, and for each successive event his next partner is the next name on his card.

Couples Change

Ballroom Dances *Juniors to Adults*

The couples are all dancing. The music stops and the leader calls "All change partners." Each boy then leaves his partner and secures another. The music stops for such changes frequently.

Snap the Broom

Ballroom Dances *Juniors to Adults*

If there are more boys than girls, do not permit robbing in this dance but place a broom in the center of the floor. An unattached boy is permitted at any time to step on the broom, lift the handle, and let it snap to the floor. At this signal all must change partners and the unattached boys attempt to secure partners in the exchange.

Virginia Reel Formation

Ballroom Dances, Parties   *Juniors to Adults*

The boys and girls stand in separate lines about twenty feet apart, each standing opposite and facing his or her partner. The girl at the head of the line marches diagonally to the center and is met there by the boy from the foot of the opposite line; these two are partners and go outside the line to dance. Then the boy at the head of the line goes out to meet the girl from the foot of the opposite line. Continue in this way with the corner people meeting and dancing until all have partners.

Backward Choice

Ballroom Dances, Parties   *Juniors to Adults*

Line up the girls at one end of the floor and the boys at the other, all facing the wall. As the music starts all walk backward toward the center until they touch a member of the opposite sex. Those touching are partners.

Rushes

Ballroom Dances, Parties   *Juniors to Adults*

All the boys form in line at one end of the room and the girls at the other. At the signal the boys rush to the girls, select partners and dance.

ALL-FOURS RUSH.—This is for younger groups. The boys rush to the girls on all fours.

Paul Jones Circles

Ballroom Dances   *Juniors to Adults*

The Paul Jones is a traditional device of the ballroom for changing partners. It does more than change partners, however, for when properly conducted it does much to stimulate group feeling, *esprit de corps,* and greatly adds to the joy of the dance.

The leader should participate in the dancing in directing the Paul Jones—his task will be much easier in so doing. He should call his directions in a loud clear voice, speaking decisively but not unpleasantly.

Since the primary purpose is merely to change partners, the figures should be short and should not take too much time away from the dancing.

If the tempo of the music is slow the orchestra should speed up for the Paul Jones figure and then return to the usual tempo when the dancing starts again. The music should also be played softly so that the leader's directions can be heard.

DANCE WITH THE LADY ON YOUR LEFT.—The leader calls "circle all" and the couples come into a single circle and join hands. All slide to the right one phrase of the music, left one phrase, skip to the center one phrase, and back. The instructions to the boys are then called: "Dance with the lady on your left!"

GRAND RIGHT AND LEFT.—All come into a single circle. All skip to the right one musical phrase, then to the left, then center and back. The partners face each other and join right hands. Passing right sides, the men move counterclockwise and the girls clockwise. They move forward to the next dancer, give left hands and pass left sides. They continue around the circle giving right and left hands alternately until the leader signals to stop. The boys then dance with the girls whose hands they hold.

The leader may designate to the boys and girls with whom they are to dance before the passing starts by saying "Right hand to your partner and count three (five, seven)." The boys then dance with the third (fifth, seventh) girl.

DOUBLE CIRCLE.—The boys form a circle and join hands. The girls form another circle inside. The leader says "Ladies to the right and gentlemen to the left," and the two circles thus move in opposite directions. The leader signals the circles to stop and says to the boys "Dance with the lady in front of you."

BASKET FIGURE.—Two circles are formed which move in opposite directions as in the Double Circle above. At the signal to stop, the girls with hands still joined step back under the boys' arms, each girl standing between two boys, the boys raising their joined hands to allow the girls to go under. In this formation all slide right and then left. At the signal the boys dance with the lady on the right.

TWO-DEEP FIGURE.—All form one circle and then the boys step behind their partners, forming a double circle. The leader says to the boys "Move to the right (left), and dance with the third (fifth, seventh) lady."

ACROSS THE CIRCLE.—All form a single circle and slide right and left. They then skip forward toward the center and the boys pick a lady from the other side of the circle.

LADIES' CHOICE.—The girls form a circle and the boys stand in a group in the center. The girls join hands and slide around the circle until the music stops, then rush to the center and select partners. The positions of the boys and girls may be reversed if desired.

KNEEL BEFORE YOUR LADY.—All come into a single circle. At the command "Kneel before your lady" each boy faces his partner, takes her right hand in his and drops to one knee. The girls then move clockwise, winding in and out among the kneeling boys. At the signal to stop each girl dances with the boy kneeling before her.

REVERSE CIRCLES.—All couples fall into a circle, forming a double file, and promenade around the circle. At the signal the girls turn and march in the opposite direction. At the signal the boys dance with the girls nearest them.

UNDER THE ARCH.—The boys form a line on one side of the room, and the girls on the other. The end boy and the end girl march forward and form an arch near one end by joining their hands overhead. The two lines move forward and meet, and the couples go under the arch, the girls first, and dance.

SEPARATE CIRCLES.—The boys form a circle near one end of the room and the girls form a circle at the other end. Place a girl to act as leader in the center of the boys' circle and a boy in the center of the girls'. Each circle skips or dances around the leader in the center. At the signal the leaders in the center designate one boy to leave the boys' circle, and one girl to leave the girls' circle. These two meet and dance. The leaders then designate others, and so on, until all are dancing.

HUNGARIAN ROUNDEL.—This simple folk dance, easily followed from the leader's calling, is excellent for changing partners. The dancers come into a large circle and join hands. The following figures are followed:

1. Skip right eight steps.
2. Skip left eight steps.
3. Skip to center four steps, and back four steps.
4. Skip to center four steps, and back four steps.
5. Skip right eight steps.
6. Skip left eight steps.
7. Grand right and left until signal to dance with nearest girl.

METHODS OF CUTTING IN

When there are more boys than girls, it is desirable to use some method of cutting in or "robbing" so that those without partners do not need to wait until the end of the dance to secure a partner. The leader can do much to encourage the more timid ones to go out on the floor and secure a partner.

When there are more girls than boys the robbing may be done by the girls. As a rule, however, they are more reluctant to cut in than boys and need more individual encouragement.

Robber Dance

Ballroom Dances *Juniors to Adults*

This is the simplest and commonest of the methods of cutting in. The unattached boy merely walks up to the dancing couple. If the boy dancer fails to see him the robber lays his hand on the dancer's shoulder. The boy dancer thanks his partner, bows to the one who cuts in, and leaves to secure a new partner for himself by cutting in on another couple.

Robber Introductions

Ballroom Dances   *Juniors to Adults*

When robber dances are used in a dance composed of strangers, an unfriendly feeling frequently develops from the robbing, which is most undesirable and defeating to the general success of the dance. This can be eased over somewhat by the use of introductions at the time of the robbing.

The robber approaches the couple and lays his hand on the boy's shoulder and introduces himself. The dancing boy then introduces himself, presents the robber to the girl and withdraws.

Lemon Dance

Ballroom Dances   *Juniors to Adults*

Give each unattached boy a lemon. He hands the lemon to the boy of a dancing couple and takes his partner. The boy holding the lemon then passes it on quickly to someone else.

Broom Dance

Ballroom Dances   *Juniors to Adults*

Give each unattached boy a house broom. He dances with the broom up to a couple, hands the broom to the boy and dances with the girl. The boy receiving the broom then dances with the broom and seeks a new partner.

VARIATION.—Dress the broom to represent a lady.

Dummy Dance

Dances   *Juniors to Adults*

Provide a tailor's dummy or manikin doll. The boy without a dancing partner dances with the dummy. He tags a dancing couple, gives the dummy to the boy and dances with the girl.

SCARECROW DANCE.—Provide a scarecrow with which the extra man dances.

SKELETON DANCE.—Use a black cardboard with a white skeleton painted on it in place of the tailor's dummy.

Dunce Hat Dance

Ballroom Dances   *Juniors to Adults*

Place dunce hats on the heads of the unattached boys. They secure partners by going out on the floor and placing the hat on the head of a boy and taking his partner. The boy losing his partner immediately puts the hat on another boy's head.

Occasionally a farmer's straw hat or an ordinary street hat is used in this way.

Bunny Dance

Ballroom Dances   *Juniors to Adults*

This is for an Easter dance. Give each unattached boy a toy bunny. They secure partners by cutting in on dancing couples and giving the bunny to the boy, who must seek himself a new partner by passing on the bunny.

If partners are even, select one couple and give the boy the bunny and the girl a chicken. They separate, the boy seeking a partner by passing the bunny to a boy, and the girl securing a partner by handing the chicken to a girl.

VARIATIONS.—Instead of using bunnies and chickens, use any object symbolic of the season of the dance, such as Santa Claus, cupids, valentines, hearts, turkeys, hatchets, shamrocks, and so forth.

Ball Robber Dance

Ballroom Dances   *Juniors to Adults*

Provide enough volleyballs or soft rubber balls for the extra boys or girls. They stand at the edge of the dance floor and roll the balls at the dancing couples. If the ball touches a couple, the girl dances with the boy who rolled the ball, or the boy dances with the girl who rolled the ball.

Those left without partners take the balls and roll them.

Hoop Dance

Ballroom Dances   *Juniors to Adults*

Give each unattached boy two barrel hoops wound with colored cloth or crepe paper. He goes up to the boy dancer whom he wishes to rob and gives him one hoop. The couple stops dancing and the two boys spin their hoops on the floor. The one whose hoop spins the longest claims the girl, and the other seeks to rob someone else.

Lariat Robber Dance

Ballroom Dances   *Juniors to Adults*

This is an event for a dance for younger dancers in which a cowboy atmosphere is desired. Give each unattached boy about twelve feet of light cotton rope, such as clothesline, which is made into a lariat. He seeks a girl with whom to dance by approaching a dancing couple and throwing the lariat around the girl. He then turns the lariat over to the boy he robbed and dances with the girl.

CIRCLE LARIAT DANCE.—Give each boy a lariat made of light clothesline and have them stand in a group in the center of the floor. The girls form a circle around them and march around the circle to the music. The boys attempt to lasso the girls with whom they want to dance. As soon as they succeed, they dance.

Robber Forfeits

Ballroom Dances   *Juniors to Adults*

If the make-up of the group is such that the robbing is apt to lag, it is well to speed it up by the use of forfeits. Anyone holding the object (broom, lemon, dummy, and so forth) when the music stops must pay a forfeit. (See Chapter X, "Forfeits for Social Gatherings.")

ELIMINATION DANCES

The eliminations are among the most popular of the social dance events. In this scheme one couple after another is eliminated and withdraws to the walls. This would be unfortunate were it not for the fact that the eliminated ones retain such a high level of interest in the contest and are curious to know who the lucky couple will be. A prize should always be given to the winning couple.

Lucky Number Dance

Ballroom Dances   *Juniors to Adults*

This is the simplest and commonest of all the eliminations. Write numbers on slips of paper, beginning with one and going up to the number of couples present. Each couple draws a number before the music starts. The leader holds a duplicate set of numbers in a hat.

When the music starts all dance. After a moment the music stops and the leader draws two or three numbers and calls them. The holders of these numbers withdraw. The orchestra then plays for a moment, stops, and more numbers are called. Continue until only one couple is left. Present this couple with the prizes.

VARIATION.—Give each boy an odd number and each girl an even number. Each time the music stops the leader draws an equal number of odd and even numbers. The holders of these numbers withdraw and the partners of those who withdraw get together and dance. Continue until only two are left. Present a prize to each.

Famous Character Elimination

Ballroom Dances   *Juniors to Adults*

This event ranks supreme among eliminations and may be used to excellent advantage in connection with the Famous Character Dance (page 25). The description of the Famous Character Dance should be read in this connection.

Give each couple a card on which is written the names of a movie actress and actor, for example Lionel Barrymore and Greta Garbo. Each time the music stops the leader pulls a card from his duplicate set and asks Lionel Barrymore and Greta Garbo (or whoever the card says) to withdraw from the floor.

Instead of using the names of actors the following may be used:

Famous characters of history—kings, warriors, presidents, and so forth.

Famous writers and poets.

Famous musicians.

Countries, States.

Colleges.

Names of animals.

Names of vegetables.

Names of flowers, trees.

Names of musical instruments and musical terms.

Names of articles of the household.

Names connected with Valentine's Day, Easter, New Year's, Christmas, Thanksgiving, and whatever the nearest holiday is.

Flower Elimination

Ballroom Dances   *Juniors to Adults*

This is one of the most interesting and satisfying of the eliminations. Two large bouquets of flowers are needed, each containing exactly the same number of each variety of flowers. Each bouquet should contain as large a variety of kinds of flowers as possible. If there are not enough kinds of flowers available so that there is a separate kind for each couple, two or three of a kind may be included. There should be only one of two or three kinds, however.

One bouquet is passed around and each girl takes one flower. The other bouquet is placed on the orchestra platform or other prominent place.

Each time the music stops, the leader withdraws one kind of flower, and calls its name. All couples holding that flower withdraw. The leader should hold the flower up as he calls it so that those who do not know its name may identify it by its appearance. Continue until only one flower is left; the couple holding that flower wins. The leader should be careful to see that there is only one of the variety of flower that is left to the last.

The leader then places his flowers all back in the bouquet and the bouquet is presented to the girl of the winning couple.

Playing Card Elimination

Ballroom Dances *Juniors to Adults*

Give each couple a playing card. The leader holds a deck of cards and each time the music stops withdraws two or three cards. The holders of these cards withdraw. Continue until only one couple is left.

Balloon Bursting Dance

Ballroom Dances *Juniors to Adults*

This is a hilarious affair. Give each boy a toy balloon and two feet of string. He inflates the balloon tightly and ties it to the left ankle of his girl. If possible the balloons should be inflated beforehand and handed to the boys, because of the tendency to seek an advantage by not inflating them completely. Announce that all whose balloons are not fully inflated will be eliminated.

When the music starts all dance, and attempt to step on the balloons of passing couples, and at the same time to defend their own. When a balloon is destroyed the couple is eliminated. The couple remaining on the floor longest wins the prize. Everyone must retain somewhat of a dancing position in attempting to step on the balloons—that is, they cannot stop dancing and run around stepping on balloons.

VARIATION.—Tie the balloons on the left wrists of the girls. The couples then reach out and break the balloons of the girls as they pass.

Valentine Elimination

Ballroom Dances *Juniors to Adults*

Give each guest a valentine and ask him or her to write his or her name on the back of it. The valentines are then collected. Each time the music stops, the leader withdraws a boy's valentine and a girl's and reads the names. These two come up, claim their valentines, and withdraw from the floor. The partners of those who withdraw get together and dance. Continue until only one girl and one boy are left.

Elimination by Affinities

Ballroom Dances *Juniors to Adults*

This elimination may be used as a continuation of the pairing-off dance, Affinities (page 29). Give each dancer a slip on which is written one-half of an affinity such as "Salt and" from "Salt and Pepper," or "Pork and" from "Pork and Beans." When the music stops the leader calls out the last half of an affinity and the holder of the first half withdraws. For example, he might call "Pepper" and the holder of "Salt and" would be eliminated. Those left without partners get together and dance. Continue until only one couple remains.

For a suggested list of fifty affinities which may be used in this dance, see Affinities (page 29).

Elimination by Old Sayings

Ballroom Dances *Juniors to Adults*

This dance may be used in connection with the pairing-off dance, Old Sayings (page 32). Give each dancer a slip containing the last part of an old saying, such as "Feather" from "Light as a Feather" or "Lightning" from "Swift as Lightning." When the music stops, the leader calls the first part of the old saying, and the holder of the last part withdraws. For example, he might say "Light as a" and the holder of "Feather" would be eliminated. Those left without partners when their partners are eliminated get together and dance. Continue until only one couple is left.

For a list of over fifty old sayings, see Old Sayings (page 32).

Flag Elimination

Ballroom Dances *Juniors to Adults*

Provide a collection of small flags of many nations and allow each couple to select a flag. The leader holds slips containing the names of the flags. Each time the music stops he withdraws a slip and announces that the "Germans will sit down" or whatever the nation happens to be. Continue until only one couple remains.

If enough different types of flags cannot be obtained for all the couples, two or three of a kind may be used. There should be only one of two or three flags, however, and the leader should see that one of these remains to the end.

College Pennant Elimination

Ballroom Dances *Juniors to Adults*

This is the same as the Flag Elimination described above, except that college pennants are used in place of flags. The pennants may be made by cutting out small pieces of cardboard and painting and lettering them.

Spot Light Elimination

Ballroom Dances *Juniors to Adults*

Turn out all the lights and make the room as dark as possible. One player is given a flashlight. He walks around the floor flashing his light on and off. Whenever the light falls on a dancing couple that couple is eliminated. Continue until only one couple remains.

Blind Bowler Elimination

Ballroom Dances *Juniors to Adults*

Blindfold one person and give him a volleyball. Each time the music stops he quickly rolls the ball on to the floor. Every couple hit by the ball is eliminated. Dodging is not permitted—no one may move a foot. If the ball hits one of the partners both are eliminated.

When the group becomes thinned out, line them up on one side of the floor and place the blind man in front of them. Continue until only one couple is left.

Last Couple Elimination

Ballroom Dances *Juniors to Adults*

Give the boy of each couple a bunny, Santa Claus, hatchet, valentine, or other token symbolic of the season. Each time the music stops the boys run to an indicated line and place their objects on it. The last boy placing his object on the line is eliminated, together with his partner. Continue until only one couple remains.

Chair Elimination

Ballroom Dances *Juniors to Adults*

Place two rows of chairs down the center of the floor, the chairs standing back to back. There are two fewer chairs than dancers. Each time the music stops all rush for a chair and sit down. *Each boy must find a chair so that a girl is sitting on his right.* The boy and girl who do not find seats are eliminated. If some of the boys and girls are not sitting alternately, those left without seats may order them to rearrange themselves, and may attempt to get to their seats in the course of the transfer.

When the music starts, two more chairs are removed and each boy dances with the girl on his right. Continue until only one couple remains.

Good Resolutions Elimination

Ballroom Dances   *Juniors to Adults*

This is particularly appropriate for New Year's Eve. Write on slips of paper, typical New Year resolutions and give one to each couple. The leader retains a duplicate set.

Each time the music stops the leader draws a resolution and reads it. The couple holding that resolution withdraws. Continue until only one couple remains.

This dance has many possibilities for entertainment if the resolutions are cleverly written and the leader is clever in calling them.

Blindman's Elimination

Ballroom Dances   *Juniors to Adults*

Blindfold two or three boys. While the couples are dancing the blinded ones move about the floor attempting to touch the dancers. Any couple touched is eliminated. As the crowd thins out, limit the dancing to one section of the floor. Continue until only one couple remains.

This is less satisfactory than some of the other methods because of the ease with which the dancers may move away from the blindfolded taggers.

Elimination by Sections of the Floor

Ballroom Dances   *Juniors to Adults*

When numbers are large the usual methods of elimination are often too long drawn out. In these cases large numbers may be eliminated at a time by eliminating all who stand on one section of the floor. Narrow lines may be painted on the floor with chalk, and each section numbered. The leader puts these numbers on slips, and each time the music stops, draws a number and announces that all standing in that section are eliminated.

When those of one section leave, the crowd at once scatters over the entire floor. The leader puts the number of the section of the floor back in the hat after drawing it, so that it may be drawn over again. Continue until only one couple is left.

Countries of the World

Ballroom Dances   *Juniors to Adults*

This elimination is the same as Elimination by Sections of the Floor except that each section of the floor is designated as a country by hanging a flag on the wall near it. When the music stops the leader announces that "The Swedes are defeated (or whatever country it is)." All dancing in the Sweden section withdraw.

COLLEGE ELIMINATION.—Each section of the floor is designated as a college by hanging a college pennant on the wall near it.

MISCELLANEOUS DANCING AIDS

Lucky Spot Dance

Ballroom Dances   *Juniors to Adults*

The leader selects five or six spots on the floor as lucky spots. When the music stops he announces one lucky spot and asks the couple dancing nearest to this spot to come to the orchestra. The dancing continues and when the music stops again, the leader designates another lucky spot and the couple nearest it comes to the front. Continue until all the spots have been named.

There are now five or six winning couples. All other dancers withdraw from the floor and the winning couples dance. The leader selects in his mind the lucky spot, turns his back to the dancers, and when the music stops, announces the spot. The couple nearest it wins the prize.

Poker Hands

Ballroom Dances   *Juniors to Adults*

This is an interesting continuation of the Matching Playing Cards method of pairing off. From a deck of playing cards, give each boy a black card and each girl a red card. Those who hold spades find the corresponding hearts for their partners, and those who hold clubs find the corresponding diamonds. That is, a boy holding the ten of spades dances with the girl holding the ten of hearts.

When all have found their partners the couples line up and march around the room in grand-march style. As they pass a certain spot each couple is given another playing card. This continues until all have five cards. (Since each couple had two cards to begin with, they are given three more.)

The couple holding the best poker hand wins the prize, and the couples proceed to dance. This event should be unannounced—if the players know what the idea is, they may begin to exchange cards.

Flashlight Dance

Ballroom Dances   *Juniors to Adults*

This dance is particularly interesting at camp and summer-resort dances where lighting effects are limited and all have flashlights.

The boys all carry lighted flashlights in their right hands while dancing and the house lights are turned out. The play of the flashlights on the walls and ceilings adds an interesting touch of atmosphere.

Follow the Leader Dance

Ballroom Dances *Juniors to Adults*

All the couples form in a double file with the leader and his partner at the head. The leader dances different dance steps and movements and leads the line through various figures and patterns. All watch the leader and do just as he does.

The following may be used:

Dance into a circle.

Reverse the direction and dance around the circle.

Dance into a straight line along one side of the room; the partners stand side by side, holding both hands and "skate" across the floor.

Holding inside hands, skip in a zigzag course down the floor.

Partners face each other but do not touch each other; dance in a zigzag down the floor.

Standing in place, the boys give their partners their right hands; the girls circle around their partners.

Dance into a circle and wind and unwind the serpentine.

Boys bow to girls, offer their arms and lead them to a seat.

Presenting Paper Hats

Ballroom Dances *Juniors to Adults*

Select three or four couples to dance. After a moment the host gives them fancy paper hats for themselves and also hats for a half dozen other couples. They present these hats to couples whom they select and the dancing continues. Repeat until all have hats.

Noisemakers, Confetti, Streamers

Ballroom Dances *Juniors to Adults*

Often the use of noisemakers, confetti, streamers, and the like is desirable. Younger dancers enjoy them particularly. These should be presented to the dancers in the same way that the paper hats are presented, as described in Presenting Paper Hats.

Dancing Championship

Ballroom Dances *Juniors to Adults*

Appoint a committee of three judges well informed on the technique of social dancing. They should be preferably from outside the group. When the music starts they observe the dancers to pick the best dancing couple.

The judges eliminate all those who in their estimation are not in the running. The elimination continues until there are but three or four couples remaining on the floor. From these the judges pick the winners.

While the rhythm may be of any type, dancing championships are frequently determined on the dancer's ability to waltz.

Changing Rhythm Dance

Ballroom Dances   *Juniors to Adults*

In the course of this dance the orchestra changes rhythm constantly, altering the tempo and shifting from waltzes to foxtrots. The contest centers around the ability of the dancers to adjust to the changing rhythm.

A committee of three judges watches the dancers and eliminates the poorer ones until three or four couples remain on the floor. From these they pick the winning couple.

CHAPTER IV

PARTY GAMES AND CONTESTS

FEARING that their party activities may be stigmatized as ancient and threadworn, many hosts and leaders of social recreation plan with the assumption that the old must be avoided at any cost and the new constantly sought. There is no more admirable tendency in recreational leadership than the seeking of the new and the drive toward originality, but curiously enough, many of the old activities continue to carry a greater appeal than the innovations.

The mere fact that a game is old should not throw it into the discard. The fact that it has withstood the test of time is in its favor, and is proof that it has play value. Furthermore, it makes little difference whether or not the game is historically old if it is new to the group. Each new generation finds the age-old games fresh and intriguing, and the older folk enjoy a return to the play of childhood days.

One has but to try the favorite party games of years gone by with a group of modern youth who carry the label of sophistication, to find proof sufficient that they will be played by present-day youth with all the zest of yesterday. In fact the revival of these games provides activities that in many groups appeal as innovations.

In the pages of this chapter are games that are new, and many more that are old, very old. And the old are presented without apologies, for no book of social play would be complete without them. The leader who avoids them is closing his eyes to many activities of primary value. The place where originality and creativeness play a part in handling these old activities is in the way in which the activity is presented.

In a sense the chapter title, "Party Games and Contests," is misleading—most of the chapters of this book contain games and contests usable and designed for parties. However, this chapter contains those activities of the party type which cannot be classified under special headings. They are the type of games traditionally used at parties where social dancing is not desired.

Describing the Party

Parties *Intermediates to Adults*

The host or hostess prepares beforehand a description of the party, leaving all the adjectives out and placing dashes in their place. During the party he or she asks each guest for an adjective of an uncomplimentary nature, not telling the purpose for which they are to be used. She writes these in the blank spaces in her description. Such words as *ugly, sour, outlandish, boring,* and *catty* may be given.

She then tells the guests she will read a description of the party in the words the guests have used. For example, the description at Mrs. Phillips' dinner party might start as follows:

"An *ugly* crowd of *sour* guests were gathered at the *outlandish* home of the *boring* Mrs. Phillips. A more *catty* crowd could not be imagined. The *snippy* Mrs. Phillips received the *repellent* guests in a *messy* dress. The *outrageous* dinner was so *disgusting* that the *hideous* Mr. Barrett . . ." and so on.

BLANKETY-BLANK.—For a really ludicrous story, take any short story and read it to the group, leaving out all the adjectives and some of the nouns and verbs. Whenever the reader hesitates, indicating that a word is wanted, the group supplies the missing word. The resulting story will stop the party.[1]

Murder

Parties *Intermediates to Adults*

The host takes one player aside and tells her that she is to be murdered—stabbed in the back—in the course of the evening. She is coached to scream and fall when stabbed. The host also takes another player aside and coaches him or her to do the stabbing. The one to be murdered does not know who is to do the stabbing. When the host is ready for the event, the lights are unexpectedly extinguished, a woman screams, confusion results, and after a pause long enough to allow the villain to get away from the spot, the lights are turned on.

The host immediately assembles the group, orders an investigation and insists that no one leave the room. He asks one of the group—a distinguished and clever person—to act as the prosecuting attorney. He is not appointed until after the murder. The prosecutor's task is to discover the murderer. He quizzes each person and everyone must answer truthfully. Gradually as the

[1] For a collection of stories with blank spaces, prepared for this game, see R. H. Pack, *Blankety-Blank.* New York: Minton Balch and Company, 1931.

questioning goes on the net closes on one or two and finally the guilt of the murderer is established.

This event has been tremendously popular recently; with a good prosecutor it has limitless possibilities for entertainment. A lawyer is not necessary for the prosecutor, in fact, is not always desirable, in that lawyers are often too concerned with legal and uninteresting technicalities.

The murderer must, of course, be near enough the victim to do his stabbing, but he must not hover obviously nearby all evening. He will be wise to get near only when others are also near, and good timing on the part of the light-extinguisher will help too.

No one in the group should know that this game is to be played until the murder is committed, except, of course, the murderer and his victim. The victim does not know when the event is to start until the lights go out.

VARIATION.—A sufficient number of ordinary playing cards are passed around so that each person present may draw one. In this group of cards, make certain that there are included an *ace* of spades and the *joker*.

The person drawing the ace of spades is to be the prosecuting attorney and the one drawing the joker is to be the murderer. After the drawing is completed the prosecuting attorney must make himself known and take his station beside the electric-light switch. The lights are turned out by the prosecutor and the players mill about the room until the murderer finds his victim, using discretion, of course, as he strikes him over the head or strangles him. The victim screams and falls to the floor. The prosecutor counts ten, giving the murderer a chance to escape and an opportunity for others in the room to move about, before he turns on the lights.

As different ones are called and recalled to the witness stand to be cross-questioned, all except the murderer must truthfully answer all questions. The murderer may lie in answer to any and all questions except this one: "Are You the Murderer?" The prosecutor tries to detect the murderer by cross-examination, and may ask the question "Are You the Murderer?" only three times in the course of the entire game. If by that time he has not found the criminal another attorney is appointed.

VARIATION.—Instead of having one of the group murdered, have one of the guests rush in and say that he just discovered the murdered body of a person well known to all present. The body was in the back yard. On the way in, one of the group was seen in the kitchen, panting and nervous. . . . The prosecutor builds up a web of circumstantial evidence against someone.

Adverbs

This is always a great fun-maker. One player thinks of an adverb and when he says that he is ready the group asks him to do certain things in the manner that the adverb implies.

For example, the player chooses "Furiously." The players, whose task it is to discover the adverb, take turns in asking him to do something which will indicate the nature of the adverb. One tells him to "Walk around the room in the manner of the adverb." He proceeds to walk furiously. The next asks him to "Shake hands with Mr. Black after the manner of the adverb." He shakes hands furiously. Another asks him to dance with the hefty Mrs. McGraw. He dances very furiously.

Finally the word will be guessed and the player who first names it becomes "it" and thinks of the next adverb.

Polite Conversation

Belle was taken into one side room and George into another, and each was given a subject unknown to the other. It so happened that Belle was assigned, "The latticework around Mrs. Bloomfield's rubbish pile" and George was given, "The League of Nations."

The two were then brought into the room to engage in a polite conversation with each other in which each was to endeavor to mention the assigned subject in such a way that the other would not suspect it as the subject. Such a task calls for clever wording in conversing politely and getting around to the subject in such a way as not to arouse the other's suspicions. When one thinks he has discovered the other's subject, he says, "That is your subject." If he is wrong, he loses.

Between Belle and George, this is what went on:

George: How do you do?

Belle: How do you do? Hasn't this been a pleasant evening? Dot's parties are always that way. She just seems to have what it takes. But I can't say that I can rave about this business of standing up here before everyone and making myself conspicuous, can you?

George: You don't say! I wouldn't call this being conspicuous exactly. It's just a chance to contribute our bit for the enjoyment of all, and the success of the occasion.

Belle: Really, now. Isn't that considerate of you, you're always so big hearted and ready to do your social duty. That's why you're so popular and always included. For my part, I would be more at home just conversing casually with a few of my close friends.

George: Nevertheless, every gathering, social or otherwise, must have some organization, and the gifted ones must be called upon to carry on the program. Take the congress of the United States, for example . . .

Belle: Aren't you flattering! So we're the gifted ones of this momentous occasion! Well, just the same, I still feel conspicuous, and I hate conspicuous things. Like the silver paint on Fritz's sport roadster, or the ugly picket fence around the Mount Sterling Cemetery. I suppose whoever conceived that was just performing his social duty? Or the latticework Mrs. Bloomfield has erected to cover up her rubbish pile. The rubbish would be an ornament compared to that. I feel just like Marge must feel in that purple dress over there.

George: Now, that's just like you—wandering off on to all kinds of unrelated metaphors. The point is, my dear Belle, that there must be a central figure in every gathering—the speaker in the House of Representatives, or the President in the League of Nations. How could any of these organizations operate if everyone just sat around as you wish to do and casually conversed with their friends?

Belle: That's your subject—the *League of Nations*. And you didn't name mine—mine was *the latticework around Mrs. Bloomfield's rubbish pile*.

Predicaments and Remedies

Parties   *Intermediates to Adults*

This interesting game is always popular with young and old. Divide the group into two teams and seat them on opposite sides of the room. One team presents the predicaments and the other the remedies. On the predicament side, each player whispers to the one on his left a predicament; on the remedy side, each whispers a remedy to the one on his left. Thus no player is the author of his own predicament or remedy, nor does anyone know whether the remedy will fit or not.

The first player states his predicament and the opposite player on the remedy side answers with his remedy.

Examples recorded at a recent party are:

Predicament: What would you do if your dog were sick?
Remedy: Throw a bucket of water on it.

Predicament: What would you do if the steak were tough?
Remedy: Shoot him on sight.

Predicament: What would you do if the mule balked? *Remedy:* Clean out his carburetor.

Predicament: If your car killed a man, what would you do with the body? *Remedy:* Send it to the dry cleaners.

Teakettle

Parties   *Juniors to Adults*

Dick, who has been put out of the room, is expected to return and guess what the word *teakettle* means. He comes in and is greeted with this kind of jargon:

"*Teakettle,*" I said to Jim, "I can't *teakettle* well."

"I thought you *teakettled?*"

"I can *teakettle,* but Betty *teakettles teakettle* beautifully."

"If I could *teakettle* like Betty does, I would be *teakettle* proud."

"I told Phil I would *teakettle* it if he would *teakettle* the grass, *teakettle* we agreed to both *teakettle.*"

"It saves *teakettle* much when you *teakettle* yourself."

"I should say *teakettle.*"

If you haven't guessed, *teakettle* stands for *so, sew,* and *sow.* Any words may be used which are pronounced alike, such as *in* and *inn; by, buy* and *bye; to, too* and *two; dear* and *deer; vane, vein* and *vain; rain, rein* and *reign; shoe* and *shoo; plain* and *plane; principle* and *principal; bare* and *bear.*

Coffeepot

Parties   *Juniors to Adults*

This is one of the most amusing and enjoyable of the party games. The players are seated in a circle. Bob is selected and put out of the room while the players think of some activity.

Bob then returns and asks questions of any player he chooses, which must be answered truthfully. *In asking the questions he must use the word "coffeepot" to represent the activity.*

For example, the players select "swimming." Bob might ask, "How often do you *coffeepot?*" "Do you *coffeepot* in the house?" "What time of the year do you *coffeepot?*" "Do you *coffeepot* just for fun?" "What things do you need in order to *coffeepot?*"

In answering, the players must also use the word *"coffeepot"* to represent the activity. Thus when Bob asks Ethel, "Does it cost money to *coffeepot?*" she answers by saying, "In some places you can't *coffeepot* without paying for it, but it usually costs nothing."

The questioning continues until Bob names the activity. The person who made the remark that enabled him to guess it is next to leave the room.

Occasionally the game is played by permitting the players to answer the questions only with "yes," "no," or "I don't know," but to allow them to answer in any way they choose adds much to the amusement.

VARIATION.—Instead of selecting an activity, an object is selected. When the player comes in, the players make remarks at will about the object. Suppose the piano was selected. The comments might be "*Coffeepot* sits on the floor," "*Coffeepot* is heavy," "*Coffeepot* can sing," and so forth.

The game may also be played by allowing the player to ask questions of individuals in the circle.

Telegrams

Parties   *Intermediates to Adults*

This event always registers. Each player is given a paper on which he is to write a telegram. The leader dictates ten letters which, in the order given, must be the first letters of the words in the telegram.

The interest in this stunt centers around the reading of the telegrams. Ridiculous telegrams, sure to bring laughs, result. A prize is given for the funniest and for the most serious telegram.

The following are samples of telegrams written recently at a party of high-school students. The letters assigned were O P A T W M Y E H B:

OUR PEANUTS AWFUL TASTY. WILL MATCH YOU EATING HALF BUSHEL.

OUR POCKETS ARE THREAD WORN. MAIL YOURS. EMMA'S HAVE BUSTED.

OLD PIPES ARE TREASURES. WORTH MANY YEARS ENJOYMENT. HAPPY BIRTHDAY.

OLD PANTS AT TAILORS. WILL MAIL YOUR EVENING HAT BACK.

Special subjects may be assigned for the telegrams. For instance, birthday telegrams may be written to someone known to the group; telegrams appropriate for Valentine's Day may be written, or Christmas telegrams to Santa Claus. Each one may be instructed to write a telegram to his senator at Washington.

Consequences

Parties   *Intermediates to Adults*

Social play has always had its Consequences, as far back as grandfather and great-grandfather can remember, and the most modern of social play still has Consequences.

Give each a paper and pencil with instructions to write an adjective or two describing a woman. The tops of the papers are folded down to cover the writing and they are passed on to the next in the circle, who adds a woman's name, folds the paper again, and passes it. So the paper is passed until each of the following is written:

An adjective describing a woman	What he did
A woman's name	What she said
An adjective describing a man	What he said
A man's name	The consequences
Where they met	What the world said
What she did	

The results might read like this:

"The languorous Kitty Huff met the profane but uprighteous Mr. Rasputin in the lobby of the Museum of Antiques. She wiped a speck out of her eye. He stared like an owl and whirled on his heel. She said, "Unhand me! What are your intentions?" He said, "Nertz to you." So they decided to return the pearl necklace and the world said, "Surely four out of every five have pyorrhea."

Art Consequences

Parties   *Juniors to Adults*

Papers and pencils are given to all. Each draws the head of a man, woman, or child. It is no drawback to the game if one can't draw—in fact it helps. The head drawn, the papers are folded down so that the head is covered, and only the neck shows. Each paper is then passed on to the next who draws the shoulders, folds the paper, and passes it. So the others follow, adding the waist, hips, legs, and feet.

All of which is of course preliminary to opening the completed drawings and passing them around.

Compliments and Slams

Parties   *Intermediates to Adults*

Phil is asked to leave the room and while he is out, the group decides on some object in the room. Phil then comes back in and goes up to Jane and says, "Why is the object like me?" Jane grasps the opportunity to tell Phil her opinion of him and says, "It isn't half as bright as a normal one."

Betty, however, thinks differently of Phil and when asked she says, "It's the brightest spot in the party." When Dan gets his chance he says, "It's always being put out of the house." Likewise, Dick remarks, "It goes out late every night in the week."

This gives it away and Phil figures out that they are talking about the electric light. Since it was Dick that made the remark that enabled Phil to guess, he is the next victim of the slams and compliments, and leaves the room.

What Would You Do?

Party, Club   *Juniors to Adults*

Prepare slips of paper and number them in pairs, two slips marked 1, two slips marked 2, and so forth. On one of these slips is written "What would you do if" and on the other "I would." Pass out the slips *one to each guest.* Those having slips saying "What would you do if" complete the sentence by describing a situation. Those whose slips read "I would" tell what they would do in some situation of which they may happen to think.

The leader then asks the person holding the slip numbered 1 saying "What would you do if" to read the question and the other person holding the slip numbered 1 to read the answer. Since the two people have worked independently the question and answer are in no respect related.

For example, the question might be, "What would you do if your Aunt Matilda got seasick?" and the answer, "I'd teach the pup to have better manners."

WHY AND BECAUSE.—The idea in this game is the same as the above except that one set of slips reads "Why" and the other set "Because."

Scouting for Words

Party, Club, Schoolroom, Summer Camp   *Juniors to Adults*

To say that this is an excellent contest is to put it mildly. It is one of the most completely fascinating events within the pages of this book, and is called for repeatedly by all ages from children to gray-haired adults. It is of such merit as an educational event or teaching device that it may seem that it should be classified under mental play and teaching games and contests, but the pleasure it brings is so great that it is described here as recreational play.

A set of alphabet cards is needed. Recreational leaders should possess a set of these cards not only for this event but for the many other games and contests in which they are used. Excellent ones are on the market at very low cost,[2] or homemade ones may be quickly made. In making them, use cards four by six inches in size. On each card print or paint a large capital letter, heavy enough so that it can be read at a considerable distance. The card should be thick enough so that it can be thrown easily. There

---

[2] Alphabet cards may be obtained from the Church Recreation Service, Delaware, Ohio. Each set contains two complete alphabets, each alphabet on differently colored cards.

should be two of each letter except x, y, and z, and one each of these.

Seat the players in a compact group. The leader stands in front holding the alphabet cards. Let us suppose he chooses to deal with automobiles. He flashes a letter and the player who first calls the name of an automobile beginning with that letter gets the card—the leader throws it to him. When the contest is over, the player with the most cards wins. The contest is a free-for-all affair, and all try to think of the automobile and call it first.

It is well to tell a loosely constructed narrative and flash the cards for words in the story. For example, the leader might tell of a hike down the road and flash cards for the names of the automobiles that passed. Then he might take the hikers through the woods and flash cards for the names of birds, trees, and flowers. Later he might take the hiking party into the restaurant and flash cards for the odors smelled, the food on the menu, and the utensils on the table.

Stories of surgical operations with the players calling the parts of the body which the surgeon removed are particularly popular. Biblical characters and characters of American history are also much enjoyed.

The possibilities of the contest in respect to subject matter are tremendous. The following list indicates the types of stories which may be used:

Shopping Trip. Things bought from the drug store, drygoods store, grocery store, hardware store, clothing store, photographic store, garage, butcher shop, tobacco store, etc.

Nature Hike. Names of birds, trees, animals, fish, insects, flowers, etc.

Hike Along the Highway. Animals seen in the fields, vegetables in the gardens, automobiles passed, trucks passed, popular billboard advertising phrases.

An Airplane Trip. Names of rivers flown over, mountains, countries, states, cities, capitals, lakes, capes, bays, islands.

At the Concert. Names of musical instruments in the orchestra, songs, composers, notes, etc.

At the Library. Names of authors, poets, novels, essays, poems.

At the Newsstand. Names of magazines, newspapers.

In the Art Gallery. Portraits of celebrated men of history, warriors, statesmen, presidents, kings, names of famous paintings, artists.

At the Lecture. Names of parts of speech: verbs, adjectives, adverbs, nouns, conjunctions, etc.

In the Operating Room. Names of parts of body removed, drugs, diseases, etc.

In the Garage. Names of tools, parts of an automobile, parts of a bicycle, names of makes of oil, gasoline, etc.

At the Restaurant. Odors, things to eat, drinks, desserts, table settings, etc.

At Sunday School. Characters in the Bible, books of the Bible, hymns.

Looking Through the Magazine. Names of advertisements, popular advertising phrases, etc.

In the Theatre. Names of famous actors, vaudeville stars, movie stars.

Listening to the Radio. Names of radio favorites, advertisers, announcers, programs, etc.

At the Political Convention. Names of present-day senators, politicians, governors, etc.

Around the House. Things found in the bedroom, kitchen, basement, bathroom, attic, etc.

At the Party. Names of girls, boys, articles of dress, jazz hits, refreshments.

Auditory Scouting for Words

Party, Club, Home, Schoolroom   *Juniors to Adults*

Instead of using alphabet cards as in Scouting for Words the letters are called by the leader. Seat the group in a compact manner and divide into two teams by indicating a division line.

The leader might say that he went into the hardware store and the first thing he saw was a H————. The player calling an article handled by hardware stores beginning with H, such as "hammer," "hook," or "hose," scores one point for his team.

Well-known articles having more than one word in the name may be indicated by calling both letters. For example, in the grocery store, the leader might call "C F" for "corn flakes."

Stage and Movie Celebrities

Party, Club   *Juniors to Adults*

Secure a large number of pictures of stage, moving-picture, and concert performers, the pictures to be eight by ten inches in size or larger. Seat the players in a compact group, and hold up the pictures one after another. The players call the name of the person in the picture as quickly as they recognize it, and the person first naming it correctly scores one point. The player scoring the most points wins.

VARIATION.—Number the pictures and have the players write down the names of the actors and actresses as the cards are held up.

Musical Clue

Parties   *Juniors to Adults*

Ethel is sent from the room and the group decides on something for her to do. For example, she is to go to the desk in the corner, open the lower right-hand drawer, take out the penwiper, secure a newspaper from the table, spread it on the floor before Judge Jitters, kneel on it and polish his shoes with the penwiper.

A pianist takes his place at the piano and Ethel is recalled. The music plays softly when she is far from doing the right thing and more loudly the nearer she gets. With an alert pianist, she will probably secure the penwiper and newspaper, but may have difficulty in getting on her knees before the Judge. Anyway, the group will be enjoying the process.

The Dagger

Parties   *Juniors to Adults*

This game is excellent if the group is not too large. Its peculiar appeal rests in the repetition of the words, and in the melodramatic "business" which invariably goes on as the lines are said with mock seriousness.

Prepare a cardboard dagger, and seat the players in a circle. The first player hands the dagger to the second, and the following conversation ensues with hushed and dramatic voices:

Number 1 to Number 2: Take this!
Number 2 to Number 1: What is it?
Number 1 to Number 2: A dagger!
Number 2 to Number 3: Take this!
Number 3 to Number 2: What is it?
Number 2 to Number 1: What is it?
Number 1 to Number 2: A dagger!
Number 2 to Number 3: A dagger!
Number 3 to Number 4: Take this!

The play thus continues around the circle until all have been included. Each time the question is referred back to the first player.

Then in the same way the following conversation goes around:

Did you buy it? (Shakes head.)
Did you steal it? (Nods head.)
Did you use it? (Holds hand over his heart and groans.)
Did he die? (Weeps.)
What will happen if you get caught? (Makes motion to cut the throat and a loud gurgling noise.)

Cat and Dog

Parties   *Juniors to Adults*

The players are seated in a circle. Number 1 holds two small objects such as a knife and fork, or a pencil and clothespin. Number 1 passes the knife to Number 2, saying "I found the dog." Number 2 says "The what?" and Number 1 answers "The dog."

Number 2 then hands the knife to Number 3 and the following conversation ensues:

> Two to three: "I found the dog."
> Three to two: "The what?"
> Two to one: "The what?"
> One to two: "The dog."
> Two to three: "The dog."
> Three to four: "I found the dog."

The knife is thus passed around the circle and the question in each case is referred back around the circle to Number 1.

At the same time that Number 1 sends the knife around the circle to the right, he starts the fork around the circle to the left, saying "I found the cat."

The fun, as well as the confusion, starts when the dog and cat meet and the players have to pass questions and answers in both directions. Continue until both cat and dog reach Number 1 again.

Shoe Scramble

Party, Club, Picnic   *Juniors to Adults*

We played this game when we were boys and we still play it in tuxedoed parties of adults. It is a question when we enjoyed it the most, or when it was played the more roughly.

The men all remove their shoes and place them in the center of the room, then withdraw and face the walls. The shoes are mixed up and arranged in a pile. At the signal all run for the pile, try to find their shoes, put them on, lace them up, and run back to the wall. The first to finish is the winner.

Yes, it is fair to throw unwanted shoes under the davenport or up the staircase, or to slip a box of safety matches in the toe, or to pull out the shoe strings.

Certainly, the women get their chance to play, but in a game of their own after the men are through.

Thieves

Parties   *Intermediates to Adults*

Paper and pencils to all as they are seated in the circle. Each writes down the name of any object he chooses. The papers are folded and passed around the circle.

When the leader says the word, each keeps the paper he holds. The leader turns to his right-hand neighbor and asks a question which the neighbor must answer by using the word on his paper. The neighbor then asks his right-hand neighbor a question which must be answered by the word he holds.

Something like this might be said:

Question: I hear thieves broke into your house last night. What did they break in with?

Answer: A pea shooter.

Question: Where was everybody in the house?

Answer: Using the *snuff box*.

Question: What did they find in the house?

Answer: A *baby bottle*.

Question: What did they do with the baby bottle?

Answer: Ate *salad dressing* from it.

Do This and Add Something

Party, Club   *Juniors to Adults*

All are seated in a circle. One stands in the center, points to a guest and makes a motion or says something. The person pointed to stands, repeats the motion, and adds another. The third then repeats the two motions and adds a third. So it goes around the circle.

The first guest shakes his fist under the second's nose. The second shakes his fist and sticks his tongue out. The third shakes his fist, sticks his tongue out, and hisses. The fourth shakes his fist, sticks his tongue out, hisses, and tweaks his neighbor's nose. The fifth shakes his fist, sticks his tongue out, hisses, tweaks his neighbor's nose, and yaps and howls like a hurt dog, and so on.

If anyone makes a mistake or forgets the sequence, he is out of the game.

Scavenger Hunt

Party, Club   *Intermediates to Adults*

The guests at the party had all departed for parts unknown throughout the city and countryside. Leta, who dislikes all things horsy, was going from one farmer's barnyard to another with a flashlight looking for a white horse in order that she might extract a few strands of hair from the animal's tail, hoping the while that the creature would be peaceful when the scissors were applied. Phil, who never yet had been called a stage door Johnny, stood at the rear door of the Majestic, patiently waiting for the show to end so that he could secure the picture of the chorus girl who stood second from the left in the front row.

Barbara was in more trouble than the rest—she was rummaging around the country home of the very proper Mr. McFarson, looking for that gentleman's tooth brush, when who should walk in but McFarson himself!

All was explained, however, when it became known that a scavenger hunt was on. Each guest had drawn from a hat a list naming ten articles which were to be gathered in the course of the evening, with instructions that in order to be in the running for the prize, all must be back with the articles by ten o'clock. No two lists were alike. To make matters worse, they had been told that nothing could be purchased, but all must be located by way of the scavenger route. Two guests (boy and girl) were allowed to work together, but no more.

Everybody returned on time and with a reasonable number of the specified articles, except Sam, who fell down on several counts —he had been to every hotel in town and just couldn't find any peppermint-flavored toothpicks, nor could he find a sound turnip, let alone a partially decayed one. Furthermore, none of the friends on whom he called had a used corn plaster lying around; the night crawlers weren't crawling that autumn night, so he couldn't capture one, and of the countless dozens of dimes he examined, not one was dated 1890.

Three of the guests returned on time with all of their articles. So these were each given another list of five articles, all three lists being the same. The one that returned first with the articles received the prize.

The following list may serve to suggest others. Remember that you will have a weird assortment of things left on your hands afterward. It is well to keep this in mind in preparing the list.

A dill pickle
A calling card—not your own
A horseshoe
A corncob
A used streetcar ticket
A head of cabbage
A stone weighing more than a half pound and less than a pound
A carrot at least five inches long
A live frog
A used garter
A theater ticket stub
A bathing suit with a hole in it
A used wick from an oil lamp
A brown derby
Some bird seed
A picture of Greta Garbo
A dog biscuit
A white chicken feather
A pair of blue overalls
A yard of lavender baby ribbon
A banana skin
A left baby slipper

A twig of evergreen
A hard-boiled egg
A barrel stave
Day before yesterday's newspaper
A monocle
An armful of hay
A pair of tin snips
A live animal other than a dog
An angleworm
A china egg
A broken mirror
Eleven mothballs
A cube of pine incense
An orange between six and seven inches in circumference

VARIATION.—Use lists containing the names of wearing apparel only, each list stating five women's garments and five men's garments. When each couple secures the articles, they put them on and return.

Co-authorship

Parties   *Intermediates to Adults*

We are going to write a discourse on the present administration in Washington; or, if the group doesn't like that, on any subject that suits them. The first guest writes down one sentence expressing his opinion, folds the paper down to cover the writing, and gives it to his neighbor, who makes his contribution. So the paper goes the rounds of all the "authors." All of which leads up to the main object of the game—the reading of the essay.

Last Will and Testament

Parties   *Intermediates to Adults*

The guests collaborate in preparing a number of last wills and testaments, following the routine used in the game of Consequences. First, papers and pencils for all, with instructions to write at the top of each paper "The Last Will and Testament of." Each then writes the name of the girl who is making the will. All then fold the top of their paper down, covering up the writing and hand it to the next player to the right. Each then adds the name of a boy who, jointly with the girl, is making the will; the papers are folded again and passed on. Several players in turn then add items to be willed, folding the paper each time and handing it on. Then the next player adds the person's name to whom the articles are to be willed.

The papers are then passed around the circle until the leader gives the signal and each player then reads the will he holds.

X

Who Are You?

Parties   *Intermediates to Adults*

This game may get rough, but it's fun nevertheless. First, papers and pencils for all. Then on the back of each player, pin a slip of paper containing the name of some celebrity. The idea is to read and write down the names on the backs of everyone else and not allow the others to read your own.

One guest plasters his back up against the wall and defies all comers to dislodge him. Another lies flat on his back on the floor and tries to get a glimpse of the other's name. Still another fortifies himself with back wedged firmly in the upholstered chair and sticks menacing feet out at his combined attackers. So the scramble goes on until time is called and the lists on the cards can be compared.

Hot Potato
(*Handkerchief Circle Ball*)

Party, Club   *Juniors to Adults*

This is a fast and furious game which can be played as strenuously as one desires without damage to rugs and furniture.

Seat the players in a circle, facing in. Keep the circle of chairs compact. If there are more than twenty-five, start two games. Select one to serve as "it," and place him in the center of the circle. The players toss a handkerchief from one to another, across and around the circle. "It" attempts to touch the handkerchief and if he succeeds, the player who touched it last becomes "it."

Keep urging the players to get rid of the handkerchief quickly and keep it flying. This game will "stop the party."

Sardines

Parties   *Intermediates to Adults*

Perhaps it is the memory of the hide-and-seek days of childhood that makes this game so popular among adults.

The whole house is available. Select a bandit by drawing lots or using a childhood counting-off rhyme. The bandit leaves the room and hides while another game is being played. Then all set out in search. Upon finding the bandit, instead of making the discovery known, the finder goes into cahoots with the bandit and crawls into his hiding place with him.

The last person to find the assortment of legs protruding from under the bed or other hiding place is the winner of the booby prize.

Jack's Alive

Party, Club, Campfire   *Juniors to Adults*

This delightful little game is always popular either in the home or sitting around the campfire. A thin splinter of wood is needed, six or eight inches long. The players are seated in a circle. The leader, standing in the circle, lights the splinter, says "Jack's alive" and hands it to a player in the circle. The player says "Jack's alive" and hands it to the next player. Thus the stick is passed around and around the circle. When the fire goes out, Jack is dead, and the object is to pass the stick on while it is still burning and not let it die on one's hands. As long as there is a glow on the stick, Jack still lives, and as the spark grows fainter the passing becomes frantic.

When at last the spark goes out the person who held it at the moment is considered responsible and is given a black mark on his or her face with the charred end of the stick. For a more efficient marker, the leader may carry in his pocket a pencil on the end of which a charred cork is stuck. A goatee or mustache or similar decoration made by the cork adds to the merriment.

Jack is now lighted and started around again. When a player gets two marks on his face he must pay a forfeit. (See Chapter X, "Forfeits for Social Gatherings.")

Whistle, Whistle

Party, Club   *Juniors to Adults*

Blindfold one player and stand him in the center while all the others form a ring about him. One with a whistle sneaks up behind the blinded one and toots the whistle. The blinded one lunges toward the sound, but the blower by now is tooting from the other side of the ring. So it goes with the blinded one clutching the air and grabbing innocent members of the circle, until at last he closes his arms on the blower. He then runs his hands over him and attempts to announce his name. If wrong, he still stays in the circle; if right, he escapes further punishment and another is selected to put on the blindfold.

Eyewitness

Party, Club   *Intermediates to Adults*

Eyewitness makes an excellent game for parties. Have two or three guests enter the room, stage a scene, and commit a crime of some sort. A cardboard knife and a pop-gun may be used, a purse snatched, and a chair or two upset in the mix-up. A few remarks should be made and plenty of screaming.

After it is over, each guest is placed on the witness stand and asked to tell what happened. Curiously enough, the reports are conflicting and no one is able to tell accurately just what took place. All of the descriptions pieced together may not tell the accurate story. After all, can the eyewitness of the crime as he testifies in court be depended upon to describe exactly what happened?

Shouting Proverbs

Parties   *Intermediates to Adults*

Divide the players into two or more groups of ten or twelve players each. Each group selects a well-known proverb and assigns one word of the proverb to each player.

The first group, at the signal, shouts its proverb, each player shouting his word at the same time. The other groups try to guess the proverb. The shouting is repeated on request until it is guessed. Then the second group shouts.

For a collection of one hundred proverbs, see Split Proverbs (page 30).

SINGING PROVERBS.—Just like the above except that the proverb is sung to some familiar tune. Each player sings his one word over and over while all the other players are singing theirs.

Chinese Superiority

Party, Home, Club   *Juniors to Adults*

This game requires quick thinking and is always popular. The leader makes the following speech: "The fox is the sacred animal of China. There is only one thing superior to the fox and that is the gun, because the gun can kill the fox. There is only one thing superior to the gun and that is man because man can shoot the gun. There is only one thing superior to man and that is the fox, because the fox is the sacred animal."

The superiority of the various objects must be carefully memorized—fox, gun, man, fox. The sign of the fox is holding one's thumbs in one's ears and spreading the fingers; the sign of the gun is holding the arms up in the position of shooting. The sign of the man is standing with one's hands on one's knees.

The players are seated in a circle with "it" in the center. "It" steps in front of a player and gives the sign of one of the objects (fox, gun, man) and begins counting to ten. Before he finishes counting the player must give the sign of the immediately superior object. Thus if "it" gives the sign of the gun and the player gives the sign of the fox, he loses and becomes "it," because the man and not the fox is the immediate superior of the gun. If, however, he gives the correct sign, he wins and "it" must try again.

Fox, Gun, Hunter

Party, Home, Club   *Juniors to Adults*

This is on the order of Chinese Superiority (page 68), but is played on a team basis and the winning determined by chance. The group is divided into two teams. Each team may consist of from one to twelve players. The leader explains as follows: "There is only one thing superior to the fox and that is the gun, because the gun can kill the fox. There is only one thing superior to the gun and that is the hunter because the hunter can shoot the gun. There is only one thing superior to the hunter and that is the fox because unarmed the man cannot catch the fox." Thus the order of superiority: fox, gun, hunter, fox.

Each group selects a captain and determines which of the three it will represent—fox, gun, or hunter—and how it will represent it. At the signal, both teams simultaneously represent in any way they choose the object they selected. The one wins which represented the superior object. Thus if one team represented the fox and the other the gun, the one representing the gun wins. Of course if both teams represent the same object, neither scores. Each team then gathers around its captain and quickly determines the object it will represent next. The team scoring six points first wins.

Rock, Scissors, Paper

Party, Home, Informal Play   *Juniors to Adults*

This game may be played as a party game with the players seated in a circle or as informal play between two players.

Explain to the group that the *rock* is superior to *scissors* because rock will break scissors; *scissors* are superior to *paper* because scissors will cut paper; *paper* is superior to *rock* because paper will wrap and conceal rock.

The sign for rock is the closed fist; for scissors, two fingers held out; for paper, the hand spread out.

Select one player to serve as "it." He approaches a player and both of them hold their right hands out with clinched fists. They bring the fist down three times and on the third time give the sign of rock, scissors, or paper. If "it" gives the superior sign he exchanges places with the player; if the player gives the superior sign, "it" must try some one else. If both give the same sign they must try it over again.

This is a great favorite of children for informal play. They add the rule, however, that the winner of each attempt has the privilege of slapping the other on the wrist by holding him by the hand with one hand and slapping him on the wrist with two fingers of the other hand.

Spin the Platter

Party, Club *Juniors to Adults*

The players sit in a circle, each having a number. "It" stands in the center with a kettle cover or some similarly shaped object. "It" spins the platter on the floor and calls a number. The holder of this number jumps forward and attempts to grab the platter before it falls to its side on the floor. If he succeeds he returns to his seat; if he fails he becomes "it."

This is an interesting game and is played with enthusiasm by all ages. The leader should be careful to spread the chairs just far enough so that the distance makes it neither too easy nor too difficult to secure the platter. "It" may spin the platter any place in the circle that he desires; he may spin it far over on the opposite side of the circle from the place where the player sits whose number he intends to call.

When boys are playing, sooner or later "it" will hit upon the strategy of blocking the player who is attempting to grab the platter. This adds a rough element which boys enjoy, but usually soon becomes so rough that the playing value of the game itself is destroyed.

ARITHMETIC SPIN THE PLATTER.—The numbering of the players should begin with twenty. If "it" wants to call twenty-four he would say "8×3," or "$17 + 7$." The player must make the computation in time to catch the platter.

CATCH THE CANE.—Instead of using a kettle cover, use a section of a broomstick about thirty inches long. "It" sets the stick on end on the floor, as near vertical as possible, holds it with a finger placed on the top, and calls a number, quickly removing his finger. The stick must be caught before falling to the floor.

Advertising Phrases

Party, Club *Juniors to Adults*

By looking over the advertisements in magazines, compile a list of well-known advertising phrases and trade slogans. Seat the players in a compact group and indicate a line through the center dividing the group into two teams. Appoint one member of each team to act as scorekeeper.

The leader states a trade slogan and the player who first calls out the product it advertises scores one point for his team. The team scoring the most points wins.

Such phrases as the following may be used: "It floats," "Ask the man who owns one," "They satisfy," "Treat yourself to the best," "Time to retire."

While the phrases are well known, it is more difficult than one might imagine to call the product quickly.

Opposites

Party, Home   *Juniors to Adults*

The players are seated in a circle. The player chosen to start the game stands in front of a seated player and suddenly points to some part of his body and says "This is my (naming some part of the body other than that pointed to)." For example, the standing player says, "This is my nose" at the same time pointing to his eye. The seated player then says, "This is my eye" while he points to his nose.

If a seated player can correctly point to and name the "opposite" before the standing player can count to ten, he is allowed to keep his seat. Otherwise he must trade with the standing player.

It adds to the interest to allow the players to point to articles of clothing as well as parts of the body.

Catch the Balloon

Party, Club   *Juniors to Adults*

The players are seated in a circle *on the floor*. Have the players number off and put the highest number in the center to act as "it." "It" holds a toy balloon. He suddenly drops the balloon and at the same instant calls a number, and the holder of that number tries to catch the balloon before it touches the floor. If he succeeds, "it" tries another number. If he fails, he becomes "it." Of course if he breaks the balloon in catching it, he loses. A few extra balloons should be blown up and handy.

Compass Facing

Party, Club   *Juniors to Adults*

This is an excellent event especially if the players have been seated for a while. It serves admirably as a "stretcher" between discussions at a club meeting or similar function.

Have the players stand while the leader tells a story:

"It was a cold bitter night and the *North* wind whistled shrilly through the shutters of his *Montana* home." On hearing the word

"North" all face to the north; on hearing "Montana" all face toward that state. Likewise they face toward each direction or locality as the leader continues: "Our hero, whose home was in *Cuba,* was not used to these *northwestern* blizzards. With mingled prayers for *southern* sunshine, he cursed the day he had moved to this land of *arctic* blasts. In his hand he held a letter from his former wife in *San Francisco.* Alas, they had parted last year in *Rochester* because of a quarrel over some property in *Santa Fe.* The letter told of their wayward son who had held up a bank in *Seattle* and now was bumming his way *around the world . . ."* When "Around the world" is mentioned, the players all spin around.

The leader should tell the story in a melodramatic fashion and should encourage the players to whistle when the wind blows, shiver when it is cold, shake their fists when the hero curses the cold, show distress over the divorce of the wife, and otherwise act the story.

Our House Is Falling Down

Parties   *Juniors to Adults*

This is a social adaptation of games of the type of Black and White, and Crows and Cranes. A large room is advantageous.

Divide the players into two groups. Each group gets together and selects a part of a house or a furnishing of a house, which is to be symbolized by the first letter of its name. The two teams line up at opposite ends of the room and then advance until within five or six feet of each other. Suppose that Team 1 selected the word "Beam." The captain would say, "Our house is falling down for want of a B." The other side then names words connected with a house which begin with B, such as bed, bedroom, bath, bedspread, basement, and so on. When "Beam" is named, the players of Team 1 run back to their wall and the players of Team 2 chase them and attempt to tag them. All who are tagged join Team 2, or if desired, a score may be kept of those tagged.

Repeat with Team 2 giving the letter.

Earth, Air, Fire, and Water

Party, Club   *Juniors to Adults*

This ancient game still holds its own as one of the most dependable of the social games. Seat the players in a circle with "it" standing in the center. "It" holds a knotted handkerchief or rolled newspaper. He tosses the handkerchief on someone's lap and says "Earth"; before he can count ten the player must call the name of some animal which runs on the earth. If "it" had called "Air" the player would have had to name a bird that flies in the air; "Water," a fish that swims in the water. When "Fire" is called, the player must make no sound.

If the player names the creature successfully, "it" tries someone else. If the player fails he exchanges places with "it." The player who is the first to fail three times must pay a forfeit; thereafter all previous failures are forgotten and all start with a clean slate. (See Chapter X, "Forfeits for Social Gatherings.")

Since clever players rely on "cat," "catbird," and "catfish" to keep them out of difficulty, it is well to rule these three creatures out.

This game may be played on a team basis by arranging the two teams in lines facing each other. The captain of one team tosses a handkerchief to a player on the other team, and if this player cannot answer he may toss it to a teammate, but the answer must be made within the count of ten. A team scores one point each time a successful answer is made. Twenty points constitute the game.

What Is My Thought Like?

Parties   *Juniors to Adults*

The players are seated. The leader states that he is thinking about something but will not say what until later. He says to each player "What is my thought like?" The first player might say "A bluejay," the second "A patrolman," the third "Rip Van Winkle" and so on. As each answer is given the leader jots it down. When all have answered, he goes to the first and says "My thought is about my necktie. Why is my necktie like a bluejay?" The player must think quickly, and might answer "It's pretty loud." He then asks the next player why his necktie is like a patrolman, and the player might answer "Always getting on somebody's neck." The third player, comparing the necktie to Rip Van Winkle, might say "It's awfully ancient."

The interest in this event centers around the humor of the answers and in any group many clever remarks will result.

Suggestive Numbers

Parties   *Intermediates to Adults*

The group is in a circle and the leader stands in the center. He points to one and calls a number and immediately that person must answer with the event or situation which first comes to his mind. For example, the leader calls "Three" and the answer

comes "It's a crowd." "1776"—"Declaration of Independence."
"Seven"—"Come eleven." "Eighty"—"Awfully old." "Ten"—
"Nights in a barroom."

Play fast for a few minutes, but don't continue too long.

Baby Picture Contest

Parties   *Juniors to Adults*

Ask each guest beforehand to bring a picture of himself taken
during his babyhood days. Number the pictures and put them on
the wall. Give the guests paper and pencil and ask each to guess
who is who among the pictures.

Gossip

Parties   *Intermediates to Adults*

As proof of how news is distorted as it travels from mouth to
mouth, try the gossip contest. Arrange the players in a circle. The
leader whispers a brief item of news to the first player, who
whispers it to the second, and so on around the circle. No repetition
or restatement is permitted—each person whispers it but once to
his neighbor. The last player states aloud the news as he heard it.
The departure from the original is usually amazing. If the last
player's statement does not satisfy the players they may correct
it, going backward around the circle, until the original statement
is made by the first player.

GOSSIP RELAY.—Arrange the players in two rows. The leader
writes a sentence on each of two slips of paper and hands one to
the first player of each team. These players read the sentence and
hand the papers back to the leader. At the signal the sentence is
passed from player to player by whisper. When the last player
gets it he runs to the leader and whispers the sentence. The team
wins whose statement is nearest correct. In a tie, the team finishing
first wins.

Continued Story

Parties   *Juniors to Adults*

If the group is large, a selected few may perform for the amusement of all; or if small, all may participate. One starts an original
story and talks for one minute, then the next immediately takes it
up at the point where it was dropped. So the story is developed,
each adding his chapter, until the last one's turn comes, whose
duty it is to bring it to a climax and a conclusion.

With a clever group, the results will be surprising.

Uncle Joshua Died Last Night

This event is a great fun-maker for all ages. Seat the players in a circle. The leader says to his right-hand neighbor: "Do you know that my Uncle Joshua died last night?" The neighbor answers "That's too bad. How did he die?" "With one eye shut" says the first player, and closes one eye. The second player repeats the lines to the third and so on around the circle. All players now have one eye shut.

The first player then repeats the statement of his uncle's death, and says that he died "with one eye shut and his mouth awry." On the third time around, he says "With one eye shut, his mouth awry, and one foot held high." The fourth time around the line is "With one eye shut, his mouth awry, one foot held high, and waving goodbye."

The success of this event rests in the laughable positions it creates.

Tom Thumb Got Sick

All are sitting in the usual circle. The leader says to his neighbor, "Tom Thumb got sick," and the neighbor asks, "How did he get sick?" To which the leader replies, "Doing this," and begins slapping his right knee with his left hand. The neighbor then says to his neighbor, "Tom Thumb got sick," and so on around the circle.

All are now slapping their right knees. The leader then repeats the lines and slaps his left knee with his right hand. This keeps up until all are doing the following:

1. Slap right knee with left hand.
2. Slap left knee with right hand.
3. Raise left heel up and down.
4. Raise right heel up and down.
5. Nod head up and down.

I Went to Paris

The players are seated around the room. The first player says, "I went to Paris." The second says, "What did you buy?" The first one answers, "A pair of shoes," and moves his feet slightly, continuing the movement throughout the game. The second person turns to the third, and says the same thing, starting with "I went to Paris." This is continued around the circle until all are moving their feet.

On the second round the first player, when asked what he purchased, answers "A fan," and begins imaginary fanning with his right hand, at the same time keeping up movements with his feet. On the third round, the leader may say he bought a pair of gloves, and wiggles the fingers of his left hand to indicate that apparel. On the next round, the leader says he bought a pair of eyeglasses and indicates it by winking fast, at the same time keeping up all other movements. On the next round he has bought false teeth, and illustrates by opening and closing the mouth.

The game may be played much quicker by having a leader tell what purchases he made and asking the players to imitate, one at a time.

Out West

Parties   *Juniors to Adults*

The leader announces that all are going out West and each player must name some article he intends to take along. He then asks each player in the circle to name the article.

For example, one might say that he intends to take his pajamas, another his pipe, another his baby carriage, and so on. The leader then asks the first player what he intends to do with his article out West. The first player then might say that he intends to sleep in his pajamas. The second player must then say that he intends to sleep in his pipe, the third that he will sleep in his baby carriage, and so on around the circle.

The second player then says that he intends to smoke his pipe, and the third must follow by saying that he intends to smoke his baby carriage.

Grabit

Party, Club   *Juniors to Adults*

Divide the group into two teams, one the destroyers and the other the defenders. A toy balloon is tossed up between them. The destroyers try to break the balloon by grabbing it, clapping the hands together on it, or stepping on it, while the defenders attempt to protect it by batting it out of reach. Keep the time required by the destroyers to break the balloon. When the balloon is broken, the defenders become the destroyers.

Give each team three turns at destroying the balloon. Add the times required by each team and the team wins that has the smallest total time.

Snatch the Handkerchief

Party, Club   *Juniors to Adults*

This is nothing more than Snatch Ball played in a furnished room at a social gathering. Divide the group into two teams and have them sit on opposite sides of the room. Have the players of each team number off, starting at opposite ends of the room so that the two players on each team holding the same number are diagonally opposite each other. Place a handkerchief midway between the chairs, set up in wigwam fashion.

The leader calls a number and each holder of the number runs to the handkerchief and watches for a chance to snatch it and return it to his seat before being tagged by the other. Neither can be tagged until he gets the handkerchief in his hands. Usually beginners snatch the handkerchief too quickly; experienced players manoeuver awhile. If the players take too long, however, the leader may call time and they must return to their places. The player who gets to his own seat with the handkerchief without being tagged scores one point for his side, but if he is tagged, one point is scored for the tagger's side.

PLUS-AND-MINUS SNATCH THE HANDKERCHIEF.—Arrange and number the players as above and designate one team as "plus" and the other team as "minus." The leader calls two numbers, for example, "Nine and Four." The players in the "plus" team add the two numbers to see who runs, and the players in the "minus" team subtract the numbers to determine the runner. Thus in the "plus" team, Number 13 would run, and in the "minus" team, Number 5. In other respects the game is like the above.

CHAMPION SNATCH.—Place the handkerchief as above, but arrange all the players except one in a line about fifteen feet from it. The odd player, known as the champion, stands fifteen feet on the other side of the handkerchief. The champion challenges one of the players and the two run out and proceed as in Snatch the Handkerchief. If the champion loses, he exchanges places with the player he challenged.

Catch the Feather

Parties   *Juniors to Adults*

The players all take hold of a sheet and stretch it tight. A fluffy or small feather such as is found in pillows is placed on the sheet. One player is selected as "it" and stands behind the others.

At the signal the players blow the fluffy and "it" tries to get it. If he succeeds, the player nearest him when he caught it becomes "it." No one is allowed to touch the fluffy except "it" and it may be propelled only by blowing. The fluffy must be kept in motion and not allowed to settle in the middle of the sheet and remain there.

Balloon Push Ball

Party, Club   *Juniors to Adults*

Balloon Push Ball is a strenuous but nevertheless delightful game for party and club use. Divide the group into two teams and station them at opposite ends of the room. Toss up a toy balloon in the center of the room, and the two teams rush for it and attempt to bat it to the other team's wall. The team succeeding in causing the balloon to hit the opposite wall first wins.

Keep a few extra balloons at hand, and in case the balloon is broken, throw another in at the spot without allowing the play to lag.

Blowing Football

Party, Home, Club   *Juniors to Adults*

This game is always enjoyed and is played with much enthusiasm provided the table used approximates the proper dimensions. The table should be three to four feet wide and seven to eight feet long. A longer table makes scoring difficult, and a shorter one is unsatisfactory from the health standpoint. Six inches from each end of the table and parallel to it draw a goal line with chalk. A ping-pong ball is used.

Divide the players into two teams—teams of from four to eight players are most advantageous. The teams stand or kneel at opposite ends of the table. The team "kicking off" places the ball on the table one third of the distance from their goal to the opposite goal. At the signal they blow the ball and the opponents blow it back. The ball thus see-saws back and forth until one team succeeds in blowing it over the opponent's goal line. If it goes off the table over the side lines it is placed in the center of the table opposite the point where it went out.

The players are not allowed to reach over their goal line with their mouths. They may get their heads together, however, and attempt to concentrate the forces of their various blows. Most scoring is accomplished by allowing the ball to approach very close to their goal line, then giving it a hard puff—in this way it can be sent forward with such momentum that the opponents will have difficulty in stopping it before it crosses their goal.

The penalty for reaching over the goal line with the mouth is the giving of the ball to the opponents, who place it three inches from their goal. They thus have an opportunity for an effective blow at the offender's goal; the offenders, however, are privileged to defend against the blow and attempt to stop the ball.

Each time the ball crosses the opponent's goal line a touchdown counting seven points is scored.

Fanning Football

Party, Club   *Juniors to Adults*

Make a goal line at each end of the room and give each player a paper fan. A ping-pong ball is used. The players of each team are scattered over the entire floor, each being assigned to an area which he must not leave.

The ping-pong ball is placed in the center, and at the signal, the players attempt to blow it across the opposing goal, using either the fan or their mouths or both. Each time the ball crosses the goal a touchdown is scored.

Numbers Change

Party, Club   *Juniors to Adults*

This is an active social game which is much enjoyed. Select a player to serve as "it" and have all the others sit in a circle. Have the players number off and give the last number to "it." "It" stands in the center and calls two numbers. The holders of these numbers change seats quickly and "it" tries to secure one of the seats for himself. If he succeeds the player left without a seat becomes "it."

VARIATION.—Blindfold "it" and place him in the circle. When he calls the two numbers the holders of the numbers change places quietly and "it" tries to touch one as he changes. If he succeeds that player becomes "it."

Ducks Fly

Party, Club   *Juniors to Adults*

The leader says "Ducks fly" and all wave their arms. He then says "Dogs bark" and all bark. He then follows with "Fish crawl," "Horses fly," "Crawfish crow," "Geese cackle," and so on. Whenever a person cackles or crows or barks or makes any movement which the creature named cannot do, he is eliminated; likewise, when he fails to respond quickly with a movement or sound that the creature can make. The leader should always imitate the sound himself as soon as he makes the statement.

When used in social gatherings it is usually better to score a point against those who make a mistake instead of eliminating them. Those who receive three points pay a forfeit. (See Chapter X, "Forfeits for Social Gatherings.")

FEATHERS.—The players all hold their arms out in front and begin flapping the hands back and forth laterally at the wrists. The leader says "Roosters fly," "Wrens fly," and so forth, and the players keep their hands going. However, when he says "Mules fly" or "Pike fly," they change the flapping to an up and down motion at the wrists. Those who fail three times to make the right motion pay a forfeit.

Balloon Hoop Blow

Party, Club   *Juniors to Adults*

Suspend two barrel hoops from the ceiling so that the bottoms hang six feet from the floor. Each team is gathered around one of the hoops. At the signal each team tosses a toy balloon in the air and attempts to blow it through the hoop from either side. If the balloon falls to the floor, it may be picked up and tossed overhead with the hands, but otherwise must not be touched.

The team wins that puts the balloon through the hoop three times first.

How Do You Like Your Neighbors?

Parties   *Juniors to Adults*

Select one player for "it" and have the others sit in a circle. "It" stands in the center. There are just enough chairs for the seated players and none for "it."

"It" approaches one of the players and asks "How do you like your neighbors?"

"Not at all," he replies.

"Whom would you like?"

"Betty Witt and John Jeffries."

The players on either side of the player must quickly exchange places with the two named, and "it" attempts to get one of the chairs. The player questioned does not move. The one left without a seat becomes "it."

If the player says that he likes his neighbors, everyone changes seats.

Shout the Number

Parties   *Juniors to Adults*

Arrange the players in a circle and give each chair a number. The player holds the number of the chair in which he sits. Number 1, occupying the first chair, calls a number by saying, for example, "One to six," and immediately Number 6 calls another number;

for example, "Six to nine." If Number 6 hesitates or calls a number which is not represented, or calls his own number, or if the wrong person answers, the person making the mistake goes to the last chair and all move up to make a place for him.

The players who moved now have new numbers. The first player then calls a number again. All numbers must be called in rapid-fire fashion, without hesitation. The game sounds simple but in fact is confusing and the failures are many.

The place of honor goes to the player in the first chair. All try to get to that chair and retain it.

When the play has gone on in this fashion for a while, it may be made more difficult by renumbering the chairs, giving them even numbers only—two, four, six, and so on. Anyone calling an odd number goes to the foot of the line. Still later, the chairs may be given every third number.

JOHN, JACK, JIM, AND JOE.—This is exactly like the above except that the first four players are not numbered but are called John, Jack, Jim, and Joe respectively. The fifth player is Number 1. The first player, John, holds the seat of honor. He calls a number, say "John to five," and Number 5 must immediately call another; for example, "Five to Jim." Jim must then immediately call another number, such as "Jim to one." In other respects the game is like the above.

MATTHEW, MARK, LUKE, AND JOHN.—That is exactly like John, Jack, Jim, and Joe except that the first four players are called Matthew, Mark, Luke, and John.

Scoot

(*Cover the Stool, Shifting Seats*)

Parties   *Juniors to Adults*

This fast-moving game appeals particularly to younger players. The players are seated in a circle. Select one to serve as "it." He stands in the circle and leaves his chair empty. "It" commands "Shift to the right," whereupon the person on whose right is the empty chair shifts to it, and the next person shifts to the chair just vacated and so on around the circle. "It" tries to get a seat and will find that it is a difficult thing to do. Everyone does not shift at once but waits until there is a vacant seat to his right. If "it" succeeds in getting a seat the person who should have shifted to the seat becomes "it."

When the shifting to the right is going on, "it" may suddenly call "Shift to the left." In the confusion he stands a good chance of getting a seat.

Fruit Basket

Parties   *Juniors to Adults*

This favorite of years gone by scarcely needs a description. It contains much more activity than the average social game.

The players are seated in a circle, and count off by fours. All the number one's are *lemons,* the number two's *oranges,* the number three's *apples,* and the number four's *bananas.* One player is selected to serve as "it" and stands in the center. "It" names two fruits such as "bananas and oranges," whereupon all bananas and oranges quickly exchange seats. "It" tries to get a seat in the scramble. The person left without a seat becomes "it."

Any combination of fruits may be spoken. If "it" calls "Fruit Basket," everyone exchanges seats.

FLOWER GARDEN.—This is played exactly like Fruit Basket except that the players are given the names of flowers and the name for all to change chairs is "Poison Ivy."

Postman

Parties   *Juniors to Adults*

This is another old game very similar to Fruit Basket. The players are seated in a circle with the postman ("it") in the center. Each player gives himself a name of a city and announces it. The postman announces that he has a letter from St. Louis to Detroit. The players having these names quickly exchange while the postman tries to obtain one of the seats in the exchange. The one left without a seat becomes postman. When "Special Delivery" is called, everyone exchanges seats.

Musical Chairs

Parties   *Juniors to Adults*

The players are seated in a circle, facing in, with the exception of three or four who stand in the center. There are just enough chairs for those who are seated.

When the piano starts all the players including those in the center move around the circle in front of the chairs. When the music stops all scramble for a seat. Those who fail to get a seat go in the center.

MUSICAL BUMPS.—This is the same as Musical Chairs except that there are no chairs, and all march around in a circle; when the music stops all quickly sit on the floor. The last one down is eliminated. Continue until only one remains standing.

Going to Jerusalem

Parties *Juniors to Adults*

Although this ancient game may be familiar to all, its popularity demands a description.

A double row of chairs is placed in the center of the room, the rows being placed back to back, backs touching, and facing in opposite directions. There should be one fewer chair than there are players; if numbers are large there should be three or four fewer chairs than players.

The players line up and march around the chairs to the music of a piano; if no music is available, the leader may clap his hands. When the music stops the leader calls "Jerusalem" and all rush for a seat. The one failing to secure a seat falls out and takes one chair with him. The game goes on until there is only one chair left. The player who secures this one "gets to Jerusalem" and wins.

Tire Change

Lawn, Playground *Juniors to Seniors*

This is a game for a party on a lawn. A number of old automobile tires are scattered around the lawn in a rough circle. There should be a tire for each couple present. A couple (boy and girl) stand in each tire, and an odd player ("it") stands in the center.

"It" calls "Change!" and all the players leave their tires and attempt to get into another tire. In the exchange "it" tries to get in a tire. The one left without a tire is "it."

Crossing the Lake

Parties *Juniors to Adults*

This game is similar to Going to Jerusalem. A space is marked on the floor which is wider than anyone in the group can jump. The guests are asked to march around the seats and through the marked space, stopping when the whistle sounds. All those who are within the space at the signal of the whistle must drop out of the game. Of course everyone will run as quickly as possible through the space on the floor. The winner is the one left when all others have dropped out.

Poor Pussy

Parties *Juniors to Adults*

This game is particularly effective if there is a wide variety of ages in the group. Children and dignified adults of both sexes make an ideal situation.

Select a boy to serve as "pussy." He kneels before a girl and mews like a cat three times. Each time he mews the girl says "Poor pussy" and solemnly shakes her head. If the pussy can make the girl laugh or smile in the process, she becomes the pussy and kneels in front of a boy. The pussy should present a variety of types of mews accompanied by appropriate facial expressions.

Jerusalem and Jericho

Parties   *Juniors to Adults*

No collection of social games would be complete without this old-time favorite. The leader stands where all can see. The guests are all standing in an informal line, if possible. The leader calls either "Jerusalem" or "Jericho." If he says "Jerusalem" all bow deeply. If he says "Jericho" no one moves. The leader attempts to confuse by trailing out the first syllable, as "J-e-e-r-r-rusalem" or "Je-e-r-r-richo." Anyone bowing when he should not, or failing to bow quickly when he should, must exchange places with the leader.

Menagerie

Party, Club   *Juniors to Adults*

The circus sideshow barker takes his stand and in characteristic language announces the greatest animal show in the universe, concluding by saying, "Now in the first cage, ladies and gentlemen, we have the great jumbo bullfrog, the most dangerous and morose of all the bullfrogs, captured in the wilds of 42nd street. Behold the jumbo bullfrog, ladies and gentlemen!" Whereupon he points out one of the guests, who must move across the room, hopping and croaking like a frog. The barker then continues, "And now in the next cage, ladies and gentlemen, we have the rhinoceros. . . ." Continue by naming animals, birds, insects, and fishes until all have had a chance.

You Are Getting Hot

Party, Club   *Juniors to Adults*

The players are seated in a circle. One is asked to leave the room, and the players select something for him to do, such as straightening up Jack Smith's necktie. When he comes in, the players begin singing some song well known to all, singing loudly when he is far from doing the right thing, moderately when he gets "warm" and more softly the nearer he gets to touching Smith's necktie, and as he straightens it the singing dies out entirely.

Up, Jenkins!

Parties   *Juniors to Adults*

This ancient game is particularly well adapted to the dining table after refreshments have been served, but may be played sitting on the floor. The players on one side of the table constitute one team and those on the other side, the opposing team.

Give one team a coin which is passed from player to player under the table. The leader of the opposing side says "Up, Jenkins!" whereupon all players on the side having the coin raise their closed fists. The captain then says "Down, Jenkins!" and all hands are slapped down on the table with the palms spread and resting on the table.

The opposing side then goes into consultation and attempts to guess which hand conceals the coin. The captain then orders the hands raised one after the other, leaving to the last the hand under which he thinks the coin is concealed. When he orders up the coin hand he has points scored against him, one for each hand still remaining on the table. No one but the captain may order up a hand.

The coin is then given to the other side. The side loses that scores twenty-one first.

Penny Auction

Parties   *Intermediates to Adults*

Preliminary announcements instruct each person to bring a number of pennies, together with a wrapped package containing some article that he no longer needs but that may be useful to someone else. These are auctioned off without being unwrapped, by an auctioneer, with a bidding limit of ten cents.

Old Fashioned Box Social

Parties   *Intermediates and Seniors*

The age-old box social, recalled with happy memories by grand-father and grandmother, still carries an appeal. It may be used with good effect once a year to vary the program of a mixed group which meets regularly for social recreation, and incidentally will make some money for the organization. A clever auctioneer is essential to the complete success of the event.

Each girl brings a lunch wrapped in tissue paper and decorated with ribbons. No markings are on the outside to identify the owner of the package. As refreshment time approaches, the packages are stacked on a table and auctioned off to the highest bidder by the auctioneer. The boy purchasing the package eats lunch with the girl who brought it.

CHAPTER V

MYSTERY GAMES

THIS chapter presents those party games in which there is an element of mystery. The usual type is the assumption of psychic or supernatural insight on the part of one member of the group who demonstrates his ability, usually with the aid of an accomplice who is often unknown to the group. The members of the group attempt to fathom the method whereby he gets his information.

Mind Reading

Club, Party, Home   *Juniors to Adults*

This stunt is really baffling to one who does not know the method. There is no confederate or accomplice used and no trick method of communication as in the other games described in this chapter.

The performer says that he can turn his back and tell anyone which hand he puts up over his head. Someone is sure to ask for a demonstration. The performer seats this person at a table and tells him to lay his hands on the table, palms down. The performer turns his back and says "Now hold one hand up over your head." The player does this. The leader says "Now cross your feet." This the player does also. Then the leader says "If you have your feet crossed, you may lay your hand back on the table beside the other."

The player lays his hand on the table and the performer turns around, glances at the hands, looks under the table and examines the crossed feet, then points out the hand that was raised.

He is able to do this by the fact that the hand which was held over the head will be slightly pale and white as compared to the natural color of the other hand. Hold one hand overhead for a moment and compare it with the other hand, and the method will become obvious immediately.

The crossing of the feet serves two purposes. It is a device to consume time, causing the player to keep his hand in the air long enough, and it makes the trick appear complicated and thus confuses the spectators as to the method used.

Black Magic

Party, Home   *All Ages*

The leader must have an accomplice in this event. The accomplice boasts that he can leave the room and upon returning name any object that the players selected in his absence.

When the accomplice is out the players select an object and the accomplice is recalled. The leader then names one article after another, saying "Is it ———?" He finally names the selected article and the accomplice says "Yes, that is it." The correct article is the one the leader named immediately after he named a black article or one nearly black.

What Time Is It?

Home, Party   *All Ages*

The leader must have an accomplice who is sent out of the room. The group decides upon an hour of the day—six o'clock, let us say. The accomplice is called in, and as he enters he asks, "What time is it?" The leader answers. "Well, I forgot to bring my watch; I can't say exactly." The accomplice then replies "A watch isn't needed. It is six o'clock."

This trick is simplicity itself to those who are working it, but baffling indeed to the uninitiated. The key is as follows:

Hour	Key Letter	Hour	Key Letter
1	A	7	G
2	B	8	H
3	C	9	I
4	D	10	J
5	E	11	K
6	F	12	L

The first letter in the *third word* of the leader's answer tells the secret. The third word in the above example is "forgot"—"F" is the sixth letter of the alphabet, hence the hour is six o'clock.

After the stunt has been performed a few times the key may be changed by a prearranged signal between the two principals. For example, one o'clock could be represented by the letter M:

Hour	Key Letter	Hour	Key Letter
1	M	7	S
2	N	8	T
3	O	9	U
4	P	10	V
5	Q	11	W
6	R	12	X

Red, White, and Blue

Home, Party   *All Ages*

This is a trick event on the order of Black Magic, but is better in that it is more difficult to solve.

When the accomplice is recalled the leader names one article after another and the accomplice is able to pick the correct article by the following scheme: The first time he comes in it is the first article named after something red is named, the second time after something white, and the third time after something blue.

VARIATION.—Instead of referring to colors the correct object may be designated by naming it first after an object that flies, an object that cuts, or a four-legged object.

Finding the Hour

Home, Party   *Juniors to Adults*

This clever stunt is played between two people and is usable only in a very small group.

Lay a watch on the table. One player secretly selects an hour number on the face of the watch. The performer agrees to tell him the number he selected. He announces that he will begin tapping on the watch with a pencil and he asks the player to count to himself, beginning with one hour higher than the hour number he selected, and adding one to the number for each tap. When twenty has been reached, he is to say "Stop." That is, if the hour selected was six o'clock, the player would count seven to himself for the first tap, eight for the second, and so until the count has reached twenty. The performer then announces the number selected.

The method is this: The performer taps seven times any place on the watch he chooses, but on the eighth tap he starts at twelve o'clock and goes around the hour numbers counterclockwise. When the player announces that twenty has been reached, the pencil will rest on the hour selected.

The Mysterious Teacup

Party   *Juniors to Adults*

A teacup is inverted on the floor or table. A penny is placed under it. The leader leaves the room and his accomplice removes the penny and gives it to some one. The leader then returns and asks the players to put their index fingers on the cup, one after another. He then picks up the cup, places it to his ear, listens and then names the person holding the penny.

The clue is given by the accomplice in putting his finger on the cup immediately after the person who holds the penny.

Mystery City

Party, Home   *All Ages*

The leader announces that there is one in the group who possesses rare psychic powers. Among his gifts he can name the city where each was born. This person (the leader's accomplice) is sent from the room. The leader asks one player to name a city where supposedly he was born. The accomplice is called in and the leader names a number of cities, finally naming the selected city. The accomplice answers negatively to all the cities until the right one is named.

The trick is that the right city is the second city named after a two-part city. For example, the city selected is Syracuse. The leader says "Is it Miami?" "No." "Is it Los Angeles?" "No." "Is it Detroit?" "No." "Is it Syracuse?" "Yes." Syracuse is the second city named after Los Angeles, a two-part city.

The Magic Cane
(*Sign Writing*)

Party, Home   *All Ages*

The leader holds the magic cane—an ordinary cane, stick, or umbrella. He has an accomplice who is sent out of the room. The leader then asks the group to select a short verb which the accomplice can easily act out, such as walk, run, sing, or jig.

The accomplice is then called in, and with much "stage business" involving passes with the cane, taps on the floor, and comments, the leader communicates the word and the accomplice acts it out.

The leader is able to do this by a series of remarks, the first letter of each remark representing a consonant in the word. The vowels are represented by taps on the floor—A, E, I, O, and U being symbolized by 1, 2, 3, 4, and 5 taps.

Let us suppose the word was "Dance." The leader says "Do not stand too far away, Mr. Jones" (D); one tap on the floor, (A); "Now we must all be very quiet" (N); "Concentrate, my friend" (C); two taps on the floor (E).

This stunt will prove more mystifying than most such stunts.

Spirit Photography

Party, Home   *All Ages*

A player boasts that he has a magic spoon which when held before the face of anyone will record the picture of the person. The player leaves the room and his accomplice holds a shining serving spoon in front of some player, then lays the spoon on the floor in the center of the seated circle of players and returns to his seat. The player is recalled and picks up the spoon and studies it intently, finally pointing out the player photographed.

He is able to do this by watching his accomplice when he enters. The accomplice indicates by a slight movement of hand or finger which side of the circle the player is on; this eliminates half of the group. Then the accomplice assumes the exact pose of the photographed player, changing his pose as the player changes his.

It invariably happens that the accomplice will soon be asked to photograph himself. In this case the accomplice sits with his feet or legs crossed, a sign that is understood between the two.

Mystic Ashes

Parties *Juniors to Adults*

The leader holds a slip of paper for each guest present. Each is asked to name some famous person, and the leader writes the name on a slip, folds it, and places it in a hat. The slips are then shuffled, and a guest asked to draw one and keep it folded. The leader then puts the remaining slips in an ash tray and burns them. He studies the ashes, meditates, and finally states the name on the slip the guest holds. The guest opens it, and behold, the name is right!

Here is the trick: the leader writes on *every* slip the first name called. No matter which slip is drawn, it will be sure to contain the right name.

Naming the Number

Party, Club *Juniors to Adults*

The leader tells the group that one of the party with psychic powers will leave the room, and while he is out the group will select a number, and the psychic one will return and tell them the number.

When the player is recalled, the leader names a series of numbers concluding with the right number which the player recognizes, and names as the number selected.

The clue is given the player by the first number mentioned. The first digit of this number tells him what number to watch for and the second digit tells him that he is to multiply the number watched for by the second digit.

For example, the number selected is 36. When the player comes in, the leader says "59." This tells him that he is to watch for the fifth number and multiply it by nine. The leader then continues: " 84, 68, 8, 91, 4, 72, 36." The fifth number was four, which he multiplies by nine and gets 36.

The Magic Circle Is Now Begun

Party   *Juniors to Adults*

The players are seated in the circle. The leader announces that there is one present who has magic powers and will tell the name of any person with whom the leader shakes hands, even though he is out of the room and cannot see.

The leader then says, "The magic circle is now begun." Someone will be sure to say, "Really?" or "Well, you don't say." The accomplice then leaves the room knowing that the leader will shake hands with the person who first spoke after the leader said "The magic circle is now begun."

The leader shakes hands with this person and the accomplice calls out the name.

CLAIRVOYANT.—The leader must have an accomplice who is sent out of the room. The leader announces that the accomplice, even though out of the room and unable to see the group, will name the person at whom he points. The demonstrator points to an individual and calls, "Does the spirit move?" The accomplice answers, "It does. The spirit points to ——————."

The trick is that the accomplice knows that the leader will point to the last person who spoke before he left the room.

Reading Temples

Home, Party   *All Ages*

The leader must have an accomplice who is sent out of the room. The group is told that thoughts can be transmitted through feeling of one's head. The group decides on a number between one and ten and the accomplice is recalled. He places his hands on the leader's temples and after considerable "stage business" names the number.

The number is transmitted by the leader, who clinches and relaxes his jaw the required number of times. This gives a movement of the temple that can be felt but not seen.

This One, That One

Party, Home   *All Ages*

The leader has an accomplice in this event. The leader places four books on the floor in the positions illustrated in Figure 1. The accomplice knows that the books are to be named "This," "That," "This one," "That one," as shown in the diagram. The accomplice leaves the room and the group selects one book. The accomplice is then called and the leader points to a book and says

"Is it this?" "Is it that one?" and so on, until he points to a book and makes the right remark for that book.

After the first trial the names of the books are reversed "This" and "That" changing names with "This one" and "That one."

When a player thinks he has the mystery figured out, let him try it.

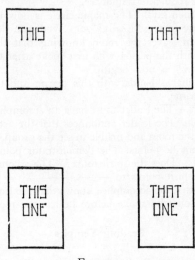

FIGURE I

The Mystifying Reader

Party, Home   *All Ages*

The guests are provided with slips of paper of the same size and shape. Each guest is asked to write a short sentence of four or five words. The words should be written plainly and not be shown to any other person. The guests are then instructed to fold the papers and they are collected by the magician who hands them to someone previously selected to act as guardian. No one, not even the guardian, should attempt to read the papers.

The guardian hands one of the papers, still folded, to the performer. The magician gravely closes his eyes, and, placing the folded paper against his forehead, remains a moment in thought. Then he calls out any sentence that has occurred to him and asks who wrote it. One of the guests, who is an accomplice, and who did not write a sentence, admits ownership of the sentence that has been announced.

The magician then unfolds the paper, apparently to verify his announcement, but his real purpose is to read the paper. He then places the paper in his left hand and reaches out to the guardian to obtain a new one. He repeats the preliminaries and then calls out the words written on the previous paper which he has had the opportunity to read. This will be a bona fide answer and one of the guests will have to admit writing the sentence. The performance is kept up in this manner until all the slips of paper have been read.

In order that the trick may be successful the accomplice must be careful to conceal from the audience the fact that he has not included a sentence in the collection given to the guardian.

Which Book

Party, Home   *All Ages*

Place six books on the floor in a row. The leader has an accomplice who is sent from the room while the group selects one of the books. The accomplice is then called in. The leader makes no remarks whatever but silently points to one book after another; the accomplice says "No" to each until the selected book is pointed out.

He is able to pick the book because he knows that the leader will point to it immediately after he points to one of the books which is next to either end.

Spirits Move

Parties   *Juniors to Seniors*

The leader's confederate remains out of the room, with the door left open so that he can hear. The leader goes from one player to another and holds his hands over the head of each, saying in each case, "The spirits move." This continues until he places his hands upon one player's head and says, "The spirits move and rest upon————." The confederate calls out the name of the person touched.

He is able to do this because of the fact that the leader touched the player in front of whom he stood when the confederate left the room.

CHAPTER VI

ROTATIVE PARTY GAMES AND CONTESTS

ROTATIVE and progressive parties are increasing in popularity tremendously, and rightly so, for there is no better device for handling an evening of games in which all are expected to participate. In this plan, several simple games are in progress at the same time in different parts of the home or hall. The players are divided into groups of four and play each game five minutes, then move on to the next. Each group thus plays all the games in the course of the evening.

In the progressive party scheme, the two highest point-winners in a game move on to the next game, and the other two remain. In the rotative party plan, all of the players move on to another game after five minutes of play at one game. *Needless to say, the rotative plan is much to be preferred.*

There are two acceptable systems of rotation which may be used:

1. Each of the groups of four is divided into two pairs of partners. When the playing period for one game is over, one pair moves on to the next game in one direction and the other pair moves to the next game in the other direction. All the players thus play all the games. The players compete for the highest individual score. This plan has the advantage of allowing each player to play with at least half of the guests present.

2. Each group of four stays intact all evening, and when the playing time for one game has expired, they move on to the next game. This plan makes it possible to compete both for the highest individual score and the highest team score. It has the further advantage of being less confusing and more easily handled than the first plan.

Which of these two plans is to be used is a matter of personal preference. The second plan described is the one developed in this chapter.

Careful planning is necessary if the rotative party is to be fully successful. There are several points which must be kept in mind in handling the preliminary arrangements and directing the play:

94

Games.—The games should be very simple, easy to understand, and require no practice. It is to the credit of the rotative party that the simplest of contests are used to the complete enjoyment of all ages of people. The group may be composed of both sexes and vary in age from eight to eighty, yet the games listed in this chapter will be played enthusiastically and prove intriguing to all concerned. Many of these games may appear childish in the reading, but one has but to try them in the rotative setting to be convinced of their appeal. To attempt the party with more complicated contests will probably mean failure.

Preliminary Arrangements.—All equipment should be at hand and the games completely set up in the place where they are to be played before the group arrives. Each game should be numbered on a large card which is hung on the wall over it, indicating the order in which the games are to be played.

Score Cards.—A score card should be prepared for each group beforehand, similar to that shown in the illustration. Each score card is numbered at the top. This number indicates to the group which game it is to start playing; that is, if a group is handed score card Number 3, it starts playing game Number 3.

ROTATIVE PARTY
Score Card No. ———

Game Number	Janet Hall	Bill Nye	Betty Gie	Joe Dodd	Total
1					
2					
3					
4					
5					
6					
7					
8					
9					
10					
TOTAL					

Teams and Captains.—When the guests arrive, divide them into teams of four and have each elect a captain. Give the captains the score cards and explain to them the method of scoring, plan of rotation, and general rules for the evening. Make the captains realize that the success of their teams will depend upon their leadership in enforcing the rules and caring for the details.

Rotation.—As soon as the teams receive their score cards they go to the games they are to start playing. Play does not start until the signal is given. After five minutes of play, the signal to stop is given, then one minute is allowed to record the scores and move to the next game. The starting signal for the next game is then given. Play must stop instantly when the stopping signal is given.

If there are ten games, the team that completes Number 10 moves to game Number 1 next.

Scoring.—Each time a player successfully completes the stunt called for in any contest he scores one point. In games where first, second, and third places are decided, first place scores three points, second place two, and third place one.

The vogue in rotative parties is to give large scores for winning. Thus one is frequently given 100 points or 1,000 points for winning a game or successfully completing the stunt that the game requires. Any number of points may be given, but for convenience in description, one point is given in the games presented below.

Make it clear that if the players play rapidly during the five minutes allowed, they will have many more opportunities to score than if they play leisurely.

The players in each group must compete in order, and in no case should a team be allowed to have its best player participate more often than the others in order to score more points for the team.

Leaders.—Rotative parties are most successful where there is a leader stationed at each game throughout the evening to explain the game and referee the play. If this is impossible, post typed rules at each game, and explain each game to the captains before the party starts.

Chair Quoits

Party, Home, Club   *Juniors to Adults*

Place a piano stool or any stool upside down so that the legs extend into the air. Failing to find a stool, a chair may be inverted on top of another chair. Rope quoits are used made as described under Rope Quoits.

The players take turns in throwing. Each throws four quoits each turn, attempting to put one on each leg of the stool. One point is scored for each leg ringed, and three points additional for ringing all four legs. The throwing line is about eight feet distant from the stool.

Bottle Quoits

Home, Party *Juniors to Adults*

Four tall-necked bottles on the order of wine bottles or quart ginger-ale bottles are needed, and also two similarly shaped pint bottles. Place the tall bottles one on each corner of a three foot square on the floor. Place the two small bottles in the center about three inches from each other, or just far enough apart so that the hoop will pass over both necks. For hoops, use six-inch embroidery hoops. Establish a throwing line ten feet or farther from one side of the square.

The players take turns in throwing, each throwing two hoops each turn. A hoop ringing one of the corner bottles, or one of the center bottles scores one point; a hoop ringing both of the center bottles scores three points.

When the contest is not used in a rotative party, twenty-one points make the game.

Fruit-Jar Ring Quoits

Home, Party, Club *Juniors to Adults*

A board six inches square and one inch thick is needed. In the center drive a large nail. Place the board on a table. Can rubbers such as are used on fruit jars are used for the quoits. The throwing line is nine to eight feet distant.

The game is played as in regular Quoits. Ringers score three points; one point is scored for each of the two rings that lie nearest the peg. Rings that do not touch the board are disregarded. Twenty-one points constitute the game.

In rotative parties, all four of the players throw one ring each, and the nearest ring scores one point. Then all throw again, and so on till the time is up.

Clothespin Ring Toss

Home, Party, Club *Juniors to Adults*

This is an excellent contest for rotative parties. In the bottom of a cardboard box insert four clothespins in a square, and in the center of the square insert a fifth clothespin. From a distance of about ten feet, toss fruit-jar rubbers at the clothespins. Each player throws five rubbers each turn. Each ringer scores one point; ringing all five clothespins scores three additional points.

Disk Quoits

Home, Party, Club   *Juniors to Adults*

Draw three concentric circles on the floor, six, twelve, and eighteen inches in diameter. From a line twelve to fifteen feet distant, slide table coasters in an effort to cause them to rest in the circles. The inner circle scores three, the next two, and the outer circle one. A coaster scores in the circle in which most of its area rests.

Washer Pitching

Party, Home, Sidewalk, Club   *Juniors to Adults*

Draw a target on the floor or sidewalk with chalk. It consists of three concentric circles, eight, sixteen, and twenty-four inches in diameter. Number the circles 3, 2, and 1. Purchase from the hardware store a dozen of the largest washers obtainable—they can probably be obtained measuring four inches in diameter. Establish a chalk throwing line twelve to fifteen feet from the target.

The players take turns in throwing or sliding the washers at the target. Each throws three washers each turn. The washer scores in the ring in which the largest portion of it rests. Twenty-one points make the game.

In rotative parties, the play continues until the time is up.

Beanbag Throwing

Party, Home, Club   *Juniors to Adults*

As physical activity, throwing beanbags at holes in a beanbag board is acceptable only for small children. As social play, it is appealing to all ages. One has but to try it with adults to be convinced. At one occasion recently a tournament was held at an outing of businessmen and was engaged in with zest and much shouting; on another occasion, a party for middle-aged women, the beanbag board was so popular the remainder of the program suffered.

There are two types of beanbag boards that may be used: The one shown in Figure 2 is twenty-four inches high and eighteen inches long, and has three round holes cut in it, the upper one four inches in diameter, the middle one five inches, and the lower one six inches. The upper hole counts three, the middle hole two, and the lower hole one.

The board illustrated in Figure 3 is twenty-four inches wide and thirty inches high. It has five triangular holes varying in size from four to eight inches, as shown in the diagram. The holes score 5, 4, 3, 2, and 1, depending on the size.

The board is set at a forty-five degree angle and the throwing line is ten feet away. Each contestant throws three bags each turn.

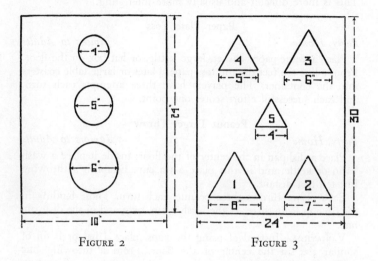

FIGURE 2   FIGURE 3

Beanbag Waste-Basket Pitch

Party, Home, Club   *Juniors to Adults*

Instead of using a beanbag board or target, set a small waste-basket or umbrella holder in the center of the room. Establish a throwing line fifteen feet distant. Each beanbag tossed into the basket scores one point. The players throw in turn, three beanbags each turn. As a party contest, this will be played by adults with enthusiasm.

Waste-Basket Throw

Party, Home, Club   *Juniors to Adults*

This little contest, characteristic of the home play of boys and girls, has been known to fascinate adults for long periods when used as a rotative-party game. It is a social adaptation of Twenty-One.

Place a waste-basket in the corner of a room. The contestants take turns in throwing for it from a line fifteen feet away. Tennis balls or soft rubber balls slightly larger are used. Each player throws three balls each turn. Each basket made scores one point.

The balls may be thrown into the basket either directly or by bouncing against the wall.

WASTE-BASKET BOUNCE THROW.—The ball must be bounced from the floor into the basket instead of thrown directly for it. This is more difficult and usually more interesting.

Paper Plate Toss

Party, Home   *Juniors to Adults*

Place a waste-paper basket, large kettle, or hat box on the floor. From a line ten feet distant, toss paper plates or large table coasters into the container. The players have three attempts each turn, and each successful effort scores one point.

Peanut Target Throw

Party, Home   *Juniors to Adults*

Place a dishpan in the center of the floor; inside it place a wash basin or kettle, and in this place a tin cup. Establish a throwing line ten feet distant.

Each player throws three peanuts each turn. Those landing in the tin cup score three; in the wash basin, two; and in the dishpan, one.

VARIATION.—Instead of using the pans, place a hat or basin of similar size in the center of the floor. From a throwing line twelve feet distant, the players in turn throw peanuts, attempting to put them in the hat. Each throws three peanuts each turn.

Umbrella Toss

Home, Party   *Juniors to Adults*

This is a very successful contest for rotative parties. Open an umbrella and place it upside down on the floor. From a line four feet distant toss a marble shooter or jack ball so that it bounces and falls in the umbrella. One point is scored each time the ball remains in the umbrella. This is difficult for the reason that the ball usually rolls out of the umbrella.

Muffin Pan Penny Toss

Party, Home, Club   *Juniors to Adults*

This little contest appeals strongly. It serves admirably in rotative parties.

An ordinary muffin pan is needed. Cut out cardboard disks and fit one into the bottom of each compartment of the pan. Set a book on end against the wall and lean the pan against it with the top edge of the pan resting on the top of the book. The pan thus sits at an angle. Draw a throwing line nine feet away from the pan. Give each player three pennies or, better still, washers of the size of pennies.

The players throw in turn, each tossing three pennies each turn. The thrower places his knees on the throwing line and may reach as far over the line as he chooses. He scores the number of points designated by the compartments of the pan in which his pennies rest.

When this is not used in the rotative party plan, the player wins who makes twenty-one first.

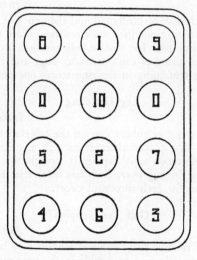

FIGURE 4

Hoop Target

Party, Home, Club   *Juniors to Adults*

This is another of those simple little contests which appear too simple in the reading, but which, when properly staged, have an appeal for all ages.

Place a wooden barrel hoop flat on the floor against a wall. Three balls are needed of different types and action, such as a baseball, a golf ball, and a tennis ball. The throwing line is ten feet distant. The players take turns in attempting to toss or roll balls into the hoop. Each player rolls all three balls each turn.

One point is scored for each ball that comes to rest in the hoop.

Calendar Toss

Home, Party *Juniors to Adults*

Place a calendar containing large numbers on a table. From a line eight feet distant toss milk-bottle tops so that they will fall on the calendar. Each top scores the amount of the number on which it rests. If the top touches two numbers it scores the amount of the higher number. Each player has three throws each turn.

Egg Roll

Home, Party *Juniors to Adults*

Cut a six-inch disk of cardboard and then cut out the center so that a cardboard ring one inch wide remains. Place the ring on a table. From a line four feet distant roll hardboiled eggs or china nest eggs, endeavoring to cause them to enter and remain in the ring. Each egg remaining in the ring scores one point.

Egg Handling

Party, Home *Juniors to Adults*

Place a china egg or rubber egg on the table with an egg cup beside it. The first player attempts to pick up the egg with a wooden mixing spoon and deposit it upright in the egg cup without tipping the cup over. Each has three tries each turn and scores one point for each successful effort.

Golf Tee Tenpins

Home, Party *Juniors to Adults*

An excellent rotative party game of tenpins may be played with golf tees. Arrange ten tees on a table in the triangular form used in Bowling. On a line about eight inches distant, place a button and snap it with the finger, endeavoring to knock down the tees. Each snaps two buttons each turn. Score as in Bowling: knocking all the tees down with one button scores a strike; all knocked down with two buttons scores a spare. (For method of scoring, see Bowling, in *Active Games and Contests*.)

Disk Roll

Home, Party, Club *Juniors to Adults*

Disk rolling contests are excellent for rotative parties. In the side of a wooden packing box, cut five upright slots one inch wide and two inches apart. From a line six feet in front of the box, roll kettle covers, hot-plate pads, or table coasters at the box in an effort to roll them through the slots into the box. The center slot scores three, the next either side two, and the end slots one. The disks must be rolled, not thrown.

Cards in the Hat

Home, Party   *Juniors to Adults*

Simple as it is, this most intriguing contest has been known to fascinate for hours. Boys and girls like to flip cards for distance and accuracy, and curiously enough adults find this pastime particularly to their liking.

Place a stiff hat on the floor in front of a chair so that when a player sits in the chair, the hat is five feet from his front foot. The player holding a pack of playing cards in his left hand places his right elbow on his right knee and attempts to flip the cards into the hat with his right hand, one at a time. The cards are not thrown, but flicked with the wrist.

The player flicks the entire deck of fifty-two cards and scores one for each card in the hat when he is finished. Cards on the brim do not count but may be knocked in by subsequent cards. First efforts are sure to be discouraging but the knack soon comes with practice.

Two players may play at once, using decks of differently colored cards.

Card Dropping

Party, Home   *Juniors to Adults*

Place a hat on the floor behind a straight-backed chair. The chair should have a rather high back. Each player is given ten playing cards. In turn, each stands in front of the chair, reaches over and attempts to drop his cards, one at a time, into the hat without touching the chair. This sounds very simple, but the cards have a way of evading the hat, and the event invariably proves intriguing.

Clothespin Drop

Party, Home   *Juniors to Adults*

Place a quart milk bottle behind a straight-backed chair. The players stand in front of the chair, reach over and attempt to drop clothespins into the bottle. Each pin dropped in scores one point.

Bean Bottle

Party, Home   *Juniors to Adults*

Place a milk bottle on the floor behind a straight-backed chair. Give each player ten beans. Each in turn stands in front of the chair, reaches over and attempts to drop the beans, one at a time, into the bottle without touching the chair. If you think it is too simple, try it.

Potato Jab

Party, Home, Council Ring   *Juniors to Adults*

Give the contestant a potato and a fork. He tosses the potato in the air and attempts to catch it on the prongs of the fork as it falls. It will be necessary to throw the potato quite high, in order to cause it to stick. Each contestant is given three attempts each turn, and each successful attempt scores one point.

Ping-Pong Bounceball

Party, Home   *Juniors to Adults*

Place an egg carton with twelve compartments on the floor. From a line six to eight feet distant, bounce a ping-pong ball on the floor, attempting to cause it to fall into the carton. To score, the ball must remain in one of the compartments. Each contestant has three attempts each turn, and each time the ball remains in the carton one point is scored.

Feeding the Elephant

Party, Home   *Juniors to Adults*

Roll a sheet of paper into a funnel with a diameter of one foot, and place it on a table. This is the elephant's mouth. About twelve feet away establish a throwing line.

The players take turns in trying to throw peanuts into the elephant's mouth. Each player is given twelve peanuts and throws three each turn. Each successful throw scores one point.

Bean Shooter Contest

Party, Club   *Juniors to Adults*

Place a pan or kettle on the floor. Provide a box of soda straws and a box of large matches. Each player takes turns in attempting to shoot matches into the pan with a soda straw used as a bean shooter. Each takes five shots each turn. The matches must remain in the pan to score. Each match so remaining scores one point.

Funnel Ball

Party, Home   *Juniors to Adults*

Provide the first player with a rubber ball and a funnel. He bounces the ball from the floor to a wall and attempts to catch it in the funnel on the rebound. He scores one point for each catch.

Ping-Pong Ball Blow for Distance

Party, Home, Indoor Council Ring   *Juniors to Adults*

This requires a smooth floor which has a straightaway of about twenty-five feet. Place a ping-pong ball on the floor at the starting line, and each in turn blows it to see who can blow it the farthest. Since the ball usually curves and starts back toward the starting line, the greatest distance it reaches away from the starting line is credited as the distance. Close the windows to keep all drafts out.

After each of the four members of a group has blown, one point is credited to the winner, then all blow again until the time is up.

Bottle Top Toss

Party, Club, Home   *Juniors to Adults*

Draw the target shown in Figure 5 on the floor. Each circle should be about ten inches in diameter. From a line fifteen feet away toss bottle tops at it. Each player throws five tops each turn. Each scores in the area in which the tops rest when all five have been tossed.

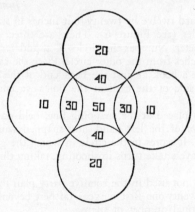

FIGURE 5

Ping-Pong Ball Roll

Party, Club   *Juniors to Adults*

Set up a stick on the floor. From a throwing line twenty feet distant, the players roll ping-pong balls at the stick, and the one wins whose ball hits or comes to rest nearest the stick. All roll one ball and the winner of each round receives one point.

False Alarm

Party, Club   *Juniors to Adults*

Hang a bell in the center of a barrel hoop and suspend the hoop vertically from the ceiling so that it is about five feet from the floor. Each player in turn throws three tennis balls, attempting to put them through the hoop without ringing the bell. Each successful throw scores one point, and each time the bell is rung one point is deducted.

Ring Catching

Party, Club   *Juniors to Adults*

Provide two canes and six small embroidery hoops. Two players hold the canes and the other two toss the rings for them from a line twelve feet distant. They try to catch the hoops on the cane. After twelve hoops have been thrown, they change places, and the throwers take the canes. Each hoop caught scores one point.

Checker Snapping

Home, Party   *Juniors to Adults*

On a cardboard twelve by twenty-four inches in size draw three concentric circles (see Figure 6). These are three, six, and nine inches in diameter. Number the circles 3, 2, and 1. The snapping line is eight inches from the outer circle. Place the cardboard on a table and place a book against the back end of the card and one against either side of the card at the bull's-eye end to stop the checkers.

A checker is placed at the snapping line, held on its side with the index finger of the left hand, and snapped with a finger of the right hand. It scores in the circle in which the greater part of it rests. The players take turns in shooting, taking three snaps each turn.

When this is not used in the rotative party plan the player wins who reaches twenty-one first or goes farthest beyond it when all have had an equal number of snaps.

Target Spin

Home, Party   *Juniors to Adults*

A top of the type spun by the fingers is needed. This may be purchased or it may be made by sawing a large spool in two and whittling it down to a cone shape. Insert a peg through the hole, sharpen the end for the point of the top, and allow the handle to extend an inch above the top. Make a target on cardboard by drawing five concentric circles, two, four, six, eight, and ten inches in diameter. Number the circles from the center out 9, 7, 5, 3, and 1, as on an archery target.

The players spin the top in turn on the target. It scores in the circle in which the point rests when it stops spinning. They continue to spin until the time is up.

When this is not used in the rotative party plan, twenty-one points make the game.

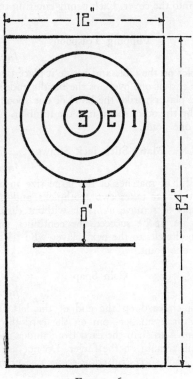

FIGURE 6

Tiddle-de-Wink Snap

Party, Home   *Juniors to Adults*

Draw a one-foot circle on a table and place a tumbler in its center. Mark four points on the table one inch outside the circle in four different directions. The players take turns in attempting to snap tiddle-de-winks into the tumbler, snapping four each turn, one from each of the four points outside the circle. Each successful snap scores one point.

Penny Roll

Party, Home   *Juniors to Adults*

Place a safety-match box cover on its side on a table with its end against a book. From a line two feet away, the players attempt to roll pennies into the cover. Each penny entering the cover scores one point.

Flipping Teaspoons

Party, Home   *Juniors to Adults*

Place a tumbler on the table and beside it place two teaspoons so that the handle end of one overlaps the handle end of the other an inch or so. The players strike the bowl of one spoon with the fist, attempting to flip the other spoon into the tumbler. Each successful attempt scores one point.

Match-Stick Jack Straws

Home, Party   *Juniors to Adults*

Place a handful of matches of the large size in a heap on the table. The first player takes two toothpicks and using them as tweezers attempts to remove a match without disturbing any of the other matches. If he succeeds he continues, but if he fails he passes the toothpicks to the next player who tries. Each match removed scores one point.

Coin Snap

Home, Party   *Juniors to Adults*

Lay a three-inch card on the end of the left forefinger and place a quarter or a smaller coin on the card directly over the finger. The stunt is to snap the card from under the coin so that the coin will still remain on the finger. Do not use a coin larger than a quarter. Each successful effort scores one point.

Cork Snap

Party, Home   *Juniors to Adults*

Place a bottle on the end of a table with the cork resting on top without being inserted. The first player stands ten feet away from the table, holds his arm out in front at full length, and walks toward the bottle, attempting to snap the cork off by snapping it with the middle finger. The palm of the hand must be kept

down and the player may not hesitate as he nears the bottle.
Each successful snap scores one point.

Hitting the Penny

Party, Home *Juniors to Adults*

This is similar to the Cork Snap. Place a penny on your forefinger and hold the hand out at arm's length in front. The player
stands ten feet away, holding a lead pencil horizontally at arm's
length in front. He *closes one eye*, walks straight toward the penny
and tries to knock it off with one blow of the pencil. The feat is
easy with both eyes open. Each successful try scores one point.

Poking the Ring.—Instead of holding a penny, a ring is held
between thumb and forefinger. The player tries to poke the pencil
through the ring.

Pointless Dart Throw

Party, Club, Home *Juniors to Adults*

Hang a six-inch embroidery hoop or a deck-tennis ring from the
ceiling. Remove the points from a half dozen darts. From a line
about ten feet away, the players take turns in throwing the six
darts, endeavoring to put them through the hoop. Someone can
hold the hoop to steady it. Each successful throw scores one point.

Shuttlecock Target Toss

Party, Club, Home *Juniors to Adults*

Draw the diagram shown in Figure 7 on the floor. From a
line fifteen or more feet distant the players take turns in throwing
a shuttlecock, endeavoring to make it fall into the scoring areas.

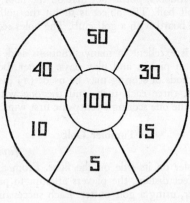

Figure 7

Shuttlecock Hoop Toss

Party, Club, Home   *Juniors to Adults*

Suspend a barrel hoop from the ceiling and, fifteen to twenty feet distant, mark a throwing line. The players attempt to throw a shuttlecock through the hoop. Each successful throw scores one point.

Party Golf

Home, Party, Club   *Juniors to Adults*

Nine small boxes or small baskets are placed about the house at considerable distance apart. They may be scattered through several rooms and even upstairs as well as down. The more "hazards" between them the better. The baskets are numbered and the "tees" marked. Each player is given a beanbag.

In true golf style, the players toss their beanbags for the first basket and then on to the remainder, keeping count of the throws. The player wins who completes the nine "holes" in the fewest throws.

In rotative parties, the winner of each hole scores one point.

PEANUT PARTY GOLF.—Place the "holes" closer together and use peanuts for balls instead of beanbags.

Golf Target-Board Putting

Party, Picnic, Home, Club   *Intermediates and Adults*

Set up a beanbag target board, constructed as described under Beanbag Throwing (Figure 2). About ten feet in front of it mark a line. If indoors, put a foot mat on the floor for a tee. Use a soft twine golf ball. The object is to hit the golf ball through the holes in the board with a golf club. The holes score three, two, and one points.

This contest is excellent in many situations aside from rotative parties, such as at picnics and play days. Under these conditions, one of two methods of scoring may be used: (1) give each player twelve attempts, three each turn, and the one with the highest score wins; (2) the one scoring twenty-one first wins.

Tumbler Golf

Party, Home   *Juniors to Adults*

Place a tumbler on its side on the floor. From a line approximately twelve feet distant, the players attempt to putt a golf ball into the tumbler, using a golf putter. Each successful effort scores one point.

Floor Golf

Party, Home *Juniors to Adults*

This is a party adaptation of Sidewalk Golf. A floor or hall providing a straightaway of twenty-five to thirty feet is needed. At each end draw a six-inch square to serve as "hole," and beside each draw a line to serve as a tee. Place a hazard or two between the holes. If space permits, several "holes" may be used, but in limited space, the players play back and forth between the two "holes."

A checker or bottle top is snapped with the middle finger, each player counting the snaps required to make the square. Each of the four players plays independently, and the one making the first hole in the fewest snaps scores one point. They then play for hole Number 2 and the winner scores one point. Continue until the five-minute period is up.

Table Golf

Home, Party, Club *Juniors to Adults*

A table with a wooden top of the size traditionally used in kitchens is needed for this popular game. With a piece of chalk draw four two-inch circles on the table to represent the holes. Also mark a tee. A checker or bottle top is placed on the tee and snapped with the finger in an attempt to put it into the first hole. The play proceeds as in Golf, the player winning who completes the circuit of the four-hole course with the fewest snaps.

The game soon loses interest unless hazards are placed on the course so that holes cannot be made in one snap. With a few minutes' work the table may be turned into a realistic golf course, making possible a most interesting parlor game. Rock hazards may be made by placing small stones on the table. Trees may be made by sticking chewing gum on the table and setting twigs in it. Hills and ridges are made with clay or putty. Streams and ponds are marked with chalk. The holes and hazards should be placed so as to make the play difficult.

Shanty Shuffleboard

Home, Party, Club *Juniors to Adults*

With chalk draw on the floor the diagram illustrated in Figure 8. The dimensions should be approximately three feet each way. The equipment needed consists of broomsticks and hot-dish pads or table coasters. Form a line twelve feet distant, slide the coasters with the broomstick in an effort to cause them to come to rest in the scoring areas. Eight coasters are used. Two players alternate in sliding them until all eight are shot. Then the score is counted and the other two players have their inning. Each coaster scores in the area in which it rests when all eight are played. Those on a line do not score.

The diagram used in Rubber Heel Toss (Figure 9) is also

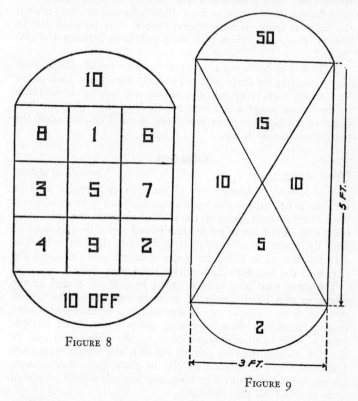

FIGURE 8

FIGURE 9

excellent for use in Shanty Shuffleboard and may be substituted for the one given here.

SHANTY TARGET SHUFFLEBOARD.—Target Shuffleboard is described in Chapter VIII, "Small Equipment Games for Club and Home." Draw the target on the floor with chalk and play with broomsticks and table coasters.

BEANBAG SHUFFLEBOARD.—Use the diagram shown in Figure 8 for the target. Toss beanbags at it, following the rules of Shanty Shuffleboard.

Parlor Shuffleboard

Home, Party, Club   *Juniors to Adults*

With chalk draw the diagram illustrated in Shanty Shuffleboard above (Figure 8). This may be put on the floor or on a table. Each square measures six inches; the design is thus eighteen inches wide.

Bottle tops or checkers are used for disks and are snapped with the middle finger from a line ten feet distant. Each player has four bottle tops. Two players alternate in snapping their four bottle tops and each top scores in the area in which it rests when the inning is over. Then the other two players have their inning.

Rubber Heel Toss

Party, Club, Home   *Juniors to Adults*

Draw the diagram shown in Figure 9 on the floor. Provide three rubber heels—used ones will do if new ones are not to be had. From a line fifteen or more feet distant, the players take turns in throwing the three heels. Each heel scores in the area in which it comes to rest. Those resting on a line do not score.

Social Ping-Pong

Party, Club   *Juniors to Adults*

A table-tennis table, two paddles, and a ball are needed. Number 1 serves to Number 2, who hits it back to Number 3, who hits it to Number 4. As soon as Number 1 serves he drops the paddle and Number 3 picks it up, and Number 1 then runs to the other end of the table. Each player in turn does likewise—hits the ball, drops the paddle, and runs to the other end of the table. When a player fails to hit the ball when his turn comes, he is eliminated. The person staying in longest scores ten points.

When not used in connection with rotative parties, the game is best played with eight players.

Swing Ball Tenpins

Party, Club   *Juniors to Adults*

Attach a soft playground ball to a rope suspended from the ceiling so that it hangs six inches from the floor. Set up the tenpins so that the king pin points away from the bowling line. The ball must swing past the tenpins and hit them on the return swing. Score ten points for each pin knocked down.

Sidewalk Bowling

Party, Yard   *Juniors to Adults*

Draw three concentric circles on the sidewalk, six, eighteen, and thirty inches in diameter. From a line twenty feet distant, roll small stones, endeavoring to cause them to come to rest in the circles. Each player bowls three stones each turn. The circles score five, three and one points.

Tin Can Pebble Toss

Party, Picnic, Playground   *Juniors to Adults*

Nail a tin can to a small board and place it on the ground. Mark out a circle around it with a six-foot radius. Mark twelve positions equally distant on the circle.

Each player holds a handful of pebbles. The first player stands at the first position on the circle and tosses three pebbles at the can. If he puts *one* of the three in he moves to the second position and throws three more. He thus continues until he misses. The other players then throw in turn, and when his turn comes again he starts from the position where he failed before.

The player wins who completes the circle when all have had an equal number of turns.

VARIATION.—When a player fails to put one of his three pebbles in the can from a certain position he must go back and start from the first position when his next turn comes. This is a more satisfactory method than the above when skillful players are competing.

PEBBLE GOLF.—Each player continues to throw from each position until he puts a pebble in the can. The throws are counted and the scoring is as in Golf.

Tire Golf

Party, Playground, Lawn, Picnic   *Juniors to Adults*

Old automobile tires are used for holes and are placed at varying distances of from 50 to 150 feet apart. Establish the first tee fifty or more feet from the first hole. The tires should be so placed that there are hazards and natural obstructions between them.

Croquet balls or playground balls are used for balls. Small children may use bean bags.

Each player in turn tosses his ball, attempting to put it in the first tire. The player winning the hole scores one point.

When this is not used in the rotative party play, score as in Golf: count the throws necessary to make each hole, and the player wins who completes the course in the fewest throws.

Hat Trimming

Parties   *Intermediates to Adults*

Select a number of couples and give each an old straw hat, some colored crepe paper, and pins. The couples trim the hat and when finished the boy puts it on. The judges pick the winners, considering both speed and cleverness in decoration.

VARIATION.—This is sometimes conducted by having the couples dress the boy from head to foot.

Lollypop Dolls

Parties   *Juniors to Adults*

Give each player (or each couple) a lollypop, some crepe paper or tissue paper of various colors, pins, pen and ink. They dress the lollypops and put faces on them. Give a small prize to the best dressed doll.

PEANUT DOLLS.—Give each a large peanut, crepe paper, pins, pen and ink, and have them turn the peanut into a doll.

CLOTHESPIN DOLLS.—Same as above, except clothespins are dressed.

Animal Modeling

Parties   *Juniors to Adults*

Give each player two or three sticks of chewing gum, a toothpick, and a card. Each chews the gum, places it on the card, and models it into an animal or bird. Worms and similar crawling creatures are ruled out. The toothpick is used to assist in the modeling and then broken up to make legs. Judges pick the winners.

If this contest is played in a home, the players should be seated at tables and carefully supervised. Otherwise gum will be unintentionally dropped on the floor and ground into the rugs.

SUITABLE ACTIVITIES FOR ROTATIVE PARTIES IN OTHER CHAPTERS

Many of the names and contests described elsewhere in this book may be used to excellent advantage in rotative parties. The slight adaptation in the rules that may be necessary occasionally can easily be made by the leader.

CHAPTER VII

MENTAL PLAY

MOST of the social games and contests are based more on mental activity than physical, and consequently there are games in practically every chapter in this book which might properly be classified under the heading of mental play. However, this chapter is limited to those games and contests of both the paper and pencil and the verbal type which call for considerable thinking and mental alertness.

The mental aspect of these games does not detract from their value as recreation, and within the pages of this chapter are to be found some of the finest of social play activities.

Hangman

Home, School, Club   *Juniors to Adults*

This interesting contest may be played in a group using a blackboard, or by two players sitting at a table and using a paper and pencil. It is an excellent educational contest and may be used in connection with any school subject. It is played with such interest that it is listed here as a quiet recreational game.

Let us suppose that the subject is automobiles. Player Number 1 draws roughly the scaffold and rope illustrated in Figure 10. He then thinks of the name of an automobile and draws a series of lines to represent the letters. For example, he selects "Pontiac" and draws the lines as follows: —— —— —— —— —— —— ——.

Player Number 2 asks "Does it have an 'e' in it?" Since it does not, his head is hung on the rope of the scaffold. He then asks "Does it have an 'i' in it?" and Number 1 writes "i" in its proper place. He then asks that the "u" be put in, but since there is none, his body is hung on his head. So it continues until he names the automobile or until he is completely hung. Since he has a head, body, two arms, and two legs, he has six chances to name the car.

If Number 2 asks that a certain letter be written in and there are two such letters in the word, both must be written. If the player names a wrong automobile he loses without further opportunity.

The best procedure to follow in guessing the word is to call the vowels first since every word is sure to have vowels in it. Knowing the vowels and the number of letters in the word, the person has information which should enable him to guess correctly.

When a group is playing, as in the case of a class in school or a club, one player ("it") is sent from the room. The group decides

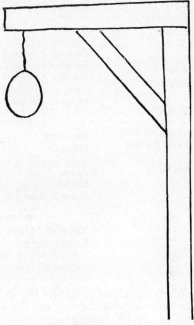

FIGURE 10

on the word and appoints a player to draw the scaffold on the blackboard, put the lines representing letters on the board and write in the letters as "it" calls them.

When used for teaching purposes, the following types of subjects may be used:

Nature	First Aid
Birds	Injuries
Trees	Diseases
Animals	
Flowers	*History*
Fish	Presidents
Fruits	Kings
Vegetables	Warriors

Famous Men
Famous Women
Famous Statesmen
Famous Battles
Famous Events

Physiology
Organs of the Body
Bones of the Body

English
Famous Authors
Famous Poets
Famous Playwrights
Poems
Famous Characters of Fiction
Famous Works of Fiction

Geography
Countries
Rivers
Mountains
States
Capitals
Cities
Lakes
Oceans

Music
Musical Instruments
Famous Composers
Musical Terms
Well-known Songs
Famous Operas

Art
Famous Artists
Famous Paintings
Famous Sculptors
Famous Statues
Famous Architectural Structures
Styles of Architecture

Chemistry
Elements
Minerals
Salts
Acids
Gases
Famous Scientists

Indian Lore
Tribes of Indians
Famous Indians
Famous Indian Battles
Articles of Indian Clothing

VARIATION.—When the subject being used involves long, difficult words, it may be better to write the first and last letters and join them with dashes for the intervening letters.

Ghost

Party, Home, Club, School   *Intermediates to Adults*

The players are seated in an informal circle. The first player calls the first letter of a word of more than two letters which he has in mind. The second player thinks of a word beginning with that letter and adds the second letter. The third player adds the third letter, and so on. Each player must be very careful that the letter he adds does not complete a word. For example, the first player calls "T," the second "R," the third "O." The fourth player, unable to think of any word but "Troy," is forced to add the "Y" and complete the word. For this he becomes a "half-ghost." Anyone who speaks to a half-ghost becomes a half-ghost. The next player then starts another word. Any player whose mistakes make him a half-ghost twice becomes a ghost. Anyone who speaks to a ghost becomes a ghost. Ghosts are out of the game, but still remain in the circle and attempt to draw the players into conversation with them.

A player must always have in mind a word of more than two letters when he calls a letter. Frequently a player, in a tight spot and unable to think of a word from the letters passed on to him, will attempt to bluff and call a letter anyway. Any player suspecting that this is the case may challenge the player to state the word he has in mind. If he is unable to do so he becomes a half-ghost; if he does name a legitimate word, the challenger becomes a half-ghost. For example, let us suppose that the letters so far named are TRINIT. The next player names the letter A. One of the other players, who expected the player to add Y and complete the word "Trinity," suspects the player of bluffing and challenges him. The player names the word "Trinitarian" and the challenger becomes a half-ghost.

A player, then, becomes a half-ghost under the following conditions:

1. If he adds a letter that completes a word of more than two letters.

2. If he speaks to a half-ghost.

3. If, when challenged, he is unable to name a legitimate word that he has in mind which is spelled by adding the letter he named.

A player becomes a ghost under the following conditions:

1. If he becomes a half-ghost twice.

2. If he speaks to a ghost.

Ghosts are out of the game.

VARIATION.—This is played just like the above except that there are three stages in becoming a ghost instead of two—one-third of a ghost, two-thirds of a ghost, and a ghost.

Cities

Party, Home *Juniors to Adults*

The first player names a city and the next player must name one beginning with the last letter of the city just given. For example, the first player calls Washington, the second New Orleans, the third Syracuse, the fourth Elmira, and so forth.

Each player must name his city before a count of ten. Those who fail are eliminated. The one wins who stays in the longest.

GHOST CITIES.—Instead of eliminating the players who fail, make them half-ghosts as in Ghost (page 118).

Twenty Questions

Home, Party, School *Juniors to Adults*

This is one of the most fascinating of the quiet games. One player ("it") thinks of some specific object anywhere in the world.

The other players then ask him questions attempting to find out what the object is. The group is allowed only twenty questions in doing so, and each question must be answered with "Yes," "No," or "I don't know." The game may sound difficult, but the object is usually named.

For example, in a recent game the questions and answers were as follows:

"Is it in the animal kingdom?" "No."
"Is it found on the American Continent?" "Yes."
"Is it confined to one particular section of the United States?" "No."
"Is its use usually confined to any particular season of the year?" "Yes."
"Is it characteristic of city life?" "No."
"Is it characteristic of rural life?" "No."
"Is it related to woods activity?" "No."
"Is it connected with a sport?" "Yes."
"Is it related to the air?" "No."
"Is it related to the water?" "Yes."
"Is it propelled by hand?" "No."
"Is it a sailboat?" "Yes."

The group defeated the one doing the answering in this ex-ample because they succeeded in naming the object with only twelve questions.

Any player may ask a question at any time. The player answer-ing keeps track of the number of questions. The player naming the object thinks of the object for the next game and is quizzed by the group.

Third Degree
(*Lawyers' Puzzle*)

Home, Party, School, Club   *Juniors to Adults*

This is a variation of Twenty Questions, but is an improvement upon it in holding interest because of the team element. This game seldom fails.

Divide the group into two or more teams of ten or twelve players each, and have each team sit in a different corner of the room. Each team selects a representative and the representatives meet and select some object from any place in the universe to be guessed. The rep-resentatives then go to a group other than their own.

The group immediately begins to shoot questions at the repre-sentative in an effort to find out the name of the object. In answer-ing, the representative may use only "Yes," "No," and "I don't know."

Suppose that the object were the dome on the capitol at Washington. The questions might start as follows: "Does it belong to the animal kingdom?" "Does it belong to the mineral kingdom?" "Is it made by man?" "Is it found in the United States?" "Is it something that most men use regularly?" "Is it found in the average household?" "Is it part of a building?" "Is its main purpose one of ornamentation?" (Read the description of Twenty Questions.)

Any number of questions may be asked. The object is to guess the object before the other teams do. Select new representatives for the next game.

Guggenheim
(*Categories*)

Party, Club, School   *Juniors to Adults*

This delightful game can be used in so many connections, and its play value is so great, that it deserves a description as a purely recreational activity.

Give each player a paper and pencil and ask each to draw the table illustrated below, or better still prepare a number of mimeographed copies of these beforehand and pass them out. Ask each to write the word "card" across the top as illustrated, or use any other four-letter word you may desire. In the compartments to the left have them write "automobiles," "cities," "countries," "flowers."

	C	A	R	D
Automobiles	Chevrolet	Auburn	Rolls Royce	De Soto
Cities	Chicago	Atlantic City	Rochester	Detroit
Countries	China	Argentina	Russia	Denmark
Flowers	Carnation	Aster	Rose	Dandelion

The idea is to write in each compartment the name of an object of the type mentioned to the left, beginning with the letter indicated at the top. Study the illustration and the idea becomes clear.

There are two methods of scoring: (1) give one point for each correct word written; (2) give ten points for each correct word that no other player has on his sheet, nine points for each word that only two players have, eight points for each word that only three players have, and so on. This encourages the players to think of unusual answers. In scoring the sheets, write the score for each word in the compartment where it is written, and then add them. The player with the highest score wins.

Any type of subject matter may be used in this game. For suggestions concerning many topics that may be used, see the list on pages 117–118.

Buzz and Fizz-Buzz

Home, Party, School   *Juniors to Adults*

This is mental play but it holds interest to such a remarkable degree for a short period that it is excellent for quiet recreational purposes. The players are seated in a circle.

There are four methods of varying difficulty which may be used:

Fizz.—The players count around the circle beginning with one, each player calling the next higher number. When five is reached "Fizz" is said instead of the number. This is also true of any number with five in it, such as fifteen, and any number that is a multiple of five, such as ten or twenty.

The fifties are handled by saying "Fizz-O," "Fizz-one," and so on. Fifty-five is "Fizz-Fizz." Each player who misses is out of the game. The one remaining in longest wins.

This may be combined with Ghost, page 118. Each player missing becomes a half-ghost, and missing twice a full ghost. The general rules of Ghost apply.

Buzz.—This is played exactly like Fizz except that "Buzz" is said in place of seven, numbers with seven in them, and multiples of seven.

Fizz-Buzz Number 1.—This is a much better form of the game for older players. It is a combination of Fizz and Buzz. "Fizz" is said in place of five, numbers containing five, and multiples of five. "Buzz" is said in place of seven, numbers with seven in them, and multiples of seven.

Fizz-Buzz Number 2.—In this form five is not considered at all. "Buzz" is said in place of seven and numbers containing seven. "Fizz-Buzz" is said for multiples of seven. Numbers which both contain seven and are multiples of seven are said by using "Buzz-Fizz-Buzz."

Buzz and Buzz-Bang.—Same as the above except that "Buzz" is substituted for seven, numbers containing seven and multiples of seven, and "Bang" is substituted for six, multiples of six, and numbers containing six.

Succotash

Home, School, Party   *Juniors to Adults*

The game is similar to Buzz and Fizz-Buzz (this page), and is derived from it.

Succotash is composed of beans and corn. The game is played in three parts—Beans, Corn, and Succotash.

Beans.—Seat the players in a circle. One player starts by saying "One," the next follows with "Two" and so on around the circle until seven is reached. In place of seven the player says "Beans." The counting continues until fourteen is reached and "beans" is substituted for this number because it is a multiple of seven. Likewise "Beans" is said for seventeen and twenty-one. In other words, "Beans" is used for every number that has seven in it or is a multiple of seven. The seventies are handled by saying "Beans-O," "Beans-one," and so on; seventy-seven is "Beans, beans."

Any player making a mistake in failing to say "Beans" at the proper time, or saying it out of place, is eliminated. Continue until eighty-four is reached (seven times twelve).

CORN.—Now we are ready for the second part. Proceed as before, substituting "corn" for nine, numbers with nine in them, and multiples of nine. Continue counting until 108 is reached (9 x 12).

SUCCOTASH.—The third and last part of the game is the real test. It combines "Beans" and "Corn." "Beans" is used for the sevens, "corn" for the nines, and "succotash" for numbers that contain both seven and nine or multiples of them. Thus twenty-seven would be "succotash" because it contains seven and is a multiple of nine. Likewise with forty-nine.

This game is no simple task for the average person and requires quick thinking, particularly when one is expected to answer promptly. A third number may be symbolized to make it more complicated, but as it is described, it is challenge enough for average groups.

I Love My Love

Party, Home   *Juniors to Adults*

In common with all alphabetical games there is much interest in this old favorite. The interest lasts but for a short time, however, and it should be followed with more vigorous play.

The first player in the circle recites the following lines, filling in the blanks with words beginning with the letter A. The second player then recites, filling in with words beginning with B, etc.

I love my love with A because he is —————— (amusing).
I will send him to —————— (Arkansas).
And feed him on ——————— (applesauce).
I will give him an —————— (atomizer to spray his nose with).
And a bunch of —————— (asters) for a nosegay.
I love my love with B because he is —————— (bulky).
I will send him to —————— (Bermuda).
And feed him on —————— (bull's brains).
I will give him a —————— (button to sew on his pants).
And a bunch of —————— (Brussels sprouts) for a nosegay.

Word Lightning

Parties   *Intermediates to Adults*

All are seated in a circle with the leader standing in the center, watch in hand. He points to a player and calls "S." The person pointed to immediately begins calling words beginning with the letter S. He may not call proper names nor, of course, repeat a word twice—he probably will repeat, either knowingly or inadvertently. The words come rapidly at first, but soon are hard to find no matter how varied a vocabulary one may have.

The words are counted for a period of one minute. Then the leader points to another and calls another letter. The player who calls the most words in one minute wins.

The Minister's Cat

Party, Home, School   *Intermediates and Adults*

This event is a challenge to one's vocabulary, but one does not need to know many words to enjoy the play. In fact, the more misses there are the more fun there is.

The players sit in a circle and each in turn describes the minister's cat with a word beginning with the letter A. For instance, the first player may say "The minister's cat is an *awful* cat," the second "The minister's cat is an *ambitious* cat," and so on. The same adjective may not be used twice. When a player cannot think of a word in a moment or so, the leader counts five slowly, and if the player has not named the adjective, he fails. Players who fail twice must pay a forfeit after the contest is over. (See Chapter X, "Forfeits for Social Gatherings.")

GHOST OF THE MINISTER'S CAT.—This is a combination of The Minister's Cat and Ghost. Each time a player fails he becomes a half-ghost or ghost as in Ghost. This makes a much better game out of it. The description of Ghost (page 118) should be read.

The King's Dinner

Party, Club, Home   *Juniors to Adults*

The leader, playing the part of the King, tells his servants that he dislikes all things beginning with a certain letter; for example, the letter T. He commands them each to suggest some food or drink for his dinner, but he will have none of it if the name contains the letter T. Any person suggesting a food or drink containing T, or who hesitates in naming an article of food, becomes a half-ghost as in Ghost, page 118. The directions for playing Ghost should be read.

For example, an acceptable menu might be pea soup, olives, fried chicken, macaroni, gravy, cabbage salad, bread and jam, coffee, and cherry pie. If a player should suggest potatoes, steak, or fruit cocktail, he would become a half-ghost because these items contain the letter T.

The letter should be changed each time the game is played.

The Ship's Record

Party, Home   *Juniors to Adults*

The players are seated in a circle with the leader in the center. The leader says to the first player, "The letter is N. The ship's name?" The player might answer "Nasturtium." The leader then says to the next player, "The ship's captain?" and the answer might be "Nelson." The next player is asked "The ship's cargo?" and the answer might be "Nuts."

"The port sailed from?" "New Orleans."

"The port bound for?" "New York."

Any player not answering before the leader counts ten slowly becomes a half-ghost as in Ghost. The description of Ghost (page 118) should be read.

Jumbled Sentences

Party, Home   *Juniors to Adults*

Give paper and pencil to all and ask each to think of a sentence, jumble the words and write them on the paper. The punctuation marks must follow the original words and all capitals must remain capitals. The papers are then passed on to the neighbor to the right, who must reassemble the words into the original sentence.

A paper might look like this:

"by heavy canyon Over sand through and mesa the gale. storm carried the swept,"

Reassembled, it reads like this:

"Over mesa and through canyon the sand storm swept, carried by the heavy gale."

Progressive Poems

Parties   *Intermediates to Adults*

Give each player a paper and pencil. Each writes a line on the paper, folds the top down, covering the writing, and hands it to his neighbor on the right, telling the neighbor the last word of the sentence. The neighbor adds a line that rhymes with the word given him. The papers are thus passed around the circle until each contains a "poem" of several lines. The players are then asked to read the poems.

Rigamarole

Parties   *Juniors to Adults*

This is a memory game which has a peculiar appeal for social play. Games which call for repetition of previous sayings are for some reason enjoyed quite universally.

The players are seated in a circle. The leader starts by saying, "One old ostrich" and each player around the circle repeats these words. Then the leader adds to the saying "One old ostrich and two tree toads twisting tendrils." This is passed around the circle as before. Each time the leader adds another phrase and each player must remember all the phrases and repeat them in order.

The saying goes around the circle ten times. As a rule, alliterative sentences of the tongue-twister type are used, similar to the following:

1. One old ostrich
2. Two tree toads twisting tendrils
3. Three tiny titmice tapping trees
4. Four fat friars fanning flames
5. Five fluffy finches flying fast
6. Six of Susie's sisters sewing shirts
7. Seven sea shells in Sarah's shawl
8. Eight elfs eating Easter eggs
9. Nine nimble noblemen nibbling nuts
10. Ten throbbing thrush thriving thither

When the rigamarole makes its last trip around the circle, each player must say, "One old ostrich, two tree toads twisting tendrils, three tiny titmice tapping trees, four fat friars fanning flames, five fluffy finches flying fast, six of Susie's sisters sewing shirts, seven sea shells in Sarah's shawl, eight elfs eating Easter eggs, nine nimble noblemen nibbling nuts, ten throbbing thrush thriving thither."

When a player makes a mistake he is eliminated. Anyone finishing without a mistake deserves all the medals in the house.

Dumb Crambo

Party, Club   *Juniors to Adults*

This old favorite combines guessing and acting, and is always popular.

Divide the players into two groups, one (the audience) which sits in chairs, and the other (the actors) which leaves the room.

The audience selects a word, either verb or noun, and the actors are recalled.

Let us suppose that the word was "sell." The actors are told that the word is a verb rhyming with "bell." The actors go into consultation attempting to guess the word which they must act out. They may think the word was "yell" and assuming the house was on fire, run around yelling "fire" and yelling in general. The audience expresses disapproval. The actors then act out "spell" by conducting school with the teacher administering a spelling lesson. Again the audience disapproves. One of the actors then comes in selling brushes and brooms and the audience claps its approval.

The audience and actors then exchange places. The side wins that acts out the word correctly in the fewest attempts.

Charades

Parties   *Juniors to Adults*

The players are divided into groups of four or five. Each group selects a word to act in pantomime and is allowed three minutes in which to prepare for it. A suggested list follows:

Automobile	Ought-oh-mob-eel
Aeroplane	Air-oh-plane
Stationary	Station-airy
Handkerchief	Hand-cur-chief
Infancy	In-fan-sea
Forswear	Four-swear
Antidote	Aunt-I-dote
Penitent	Pen-eye-tent
Cribbage	Crib-age
Masquerade	Mass-cur-aid
Bookworm	Book-worm
Knapsack	Nap-sack
Handicap	Hand-eye-cap
Pilgrimage	Pill-grim-age
Sausage	Saw-sage
Melancholy	Melon-collie
Definite	Deaf-in-ate
Pantry	Pan-tree
Bandage	Band-age
Tennessee	Ten-I-see
Catering	Kate-her-ring
Microscope	My-crow-scope
Innuendo	In-you-end-oh
Caricature	Carry-cat-your
Decorate	Deck-oar-ate
Eyelash	I-lash
Cannibal	Can-eye-ball

Ingratiate	In-gray-she-ate
Shylock	Shy-lock
Mayflower	May-flower
Pupil	Pew-pill
Penmanship	Pen-man-ship
Princeton	Prince-ton
Attenuate	At-ten-you-ate
Heroes	He-rows
Necklace	Neck-lace
Horsemanship	Horse-man-ship
Welcome	Well-come
Antarctic	Aunt-ark-tick
Buccaneer	Buck-can-ear
Charlatan	Char-lay-tan
Hornpipe	Horn-pipe
Independence	Inn-deep-end-dense
Kingdom	King-dumb
Ice Cream	I-scream
Phantom	Fan-Tom
Feline	Fee-line
Alternate	All-turn-eight
Metaphysician	Met-a-physician
Paradox	Par-o'-docks
Milwaukee	Mill-walk-key
Shakespeare	Shake-spear
Cicero	Sissy-row
Benjamin	Ben-jam-in

Acting Nursery Rhymes

Parties   *Juniors to Adults*

This event is on the order of Charades and Acting Proverbs. Divide the players into two or more groups of ten or twelve players each. Give them five minutes to prepare a dramatization or pantomime of a nursery rhyme. Each group takes its turn in presenting its dramatization while the players try to guess the rhyme.

The following nursery rhymes may be used:

Little Miss Muffet	Humpty Dumpty
Little Jack Horner	Hickery Dickery Dock
Mary Had a Little Lamb	Hey Diddle Diddle
Jack and Jill	Little Bo Peep
Old King Cole	Polly Put the Kettle On

Acting Musical Terms

Parties, Schoolroom   *Juniors to Adults*

Divide the players into groups of six or eight and have them take turns in acting out musical terms while the others watch and attempt to guess the term. Since most of the musical terms do not present an opportunity for much dramatization, very little preparation will be necessary on the part of a group and the acts will be short. This does not mean, however, that they will not be interesting.

The following terms may be used:

Sharp	Rests	Time	Major
Flat	Quarter	Notes	Minor
Scale	Half	Chord	Beat
Staff	Natural	Key	Air
Bars	Slur	Measure	Accent

Acting Proverbs

Parties   *Juniors to Adults*

This is on the order of Charades but is usually found much more interesting than Charades.

The group is divided into two groups. One group (the actors) leaves the room, and selects a proverb to act. They then return and present in pantomime a little act that will indicate the proverb, while the other group comprise the audience and attempt to guess the proverb. After it is guessed, the actors and audience exchange places.

Most proverbs present possibilities for a clever little act. This event is more than a guessing game; it often brings forth excellent and most entertaining impromptu dramatics. Some proverbs, such as "Make hay while the sun shines" can be easily acted and quickly guessed. Others present more of a challenge to both actors and audience—an example might be found in "It's the shovel that laughs at the poker."

The players should be encouraged to work out good dramatic situations involving the point of the proverb, and should be given sufficient time to think it out. With older players who have a flare for dramatics, it is wise to permit acts either in pantomime or with spoken lines.

The list of one hundred proverbs presented in Split Proverbs (page 30) *will offer many suggestions.*

Acting Song Titles

Parties   *Juniors to Adults*

Divide the players into two or more teams of ten or twelve each. One group does the acting while the others comprise the audience. The actors leave the room and select the title of a well-known song. They then return and enact the title as in Charades while the others try to guess the song. The next group then has its turn in acting.

Embarrassing Situations

Party, Club   *Intermediates to Adults*

Divide the players into groups of ten or twelve players each and give them ten minutes to decide on an embarrassing situation which they are to dramatize. Then each group in turn presents its dramatization while the others form the audience and attempt to guess the situation.

Symbolic Articles

Parties   *Intermediates to Adults*

Before the guests arrive the host places about the room the articles needed for the game. When all have arrived, each is given a paper containing a list of thoughts and asked to search about the room and find the object that represents each listed statement. Each writes opposite the statement the name of the object when he finds it. The one wins whose list is nearest correct.

The following list may be used:

1. A boy's ambition	A wooden shaving made by a carpenter's tool. On the answer list this should be written as "Shaving."
2. Commentators on the Bible	Two potatoes on a Bible.
3. Charge of the Light Brigade	Electric light bill.
4. A hairless Irish terrier with his eyes not open	An Irish potato.
5. A sower of tares	Needle and thread.
6. For gentlemen only	Suspenders.
7. Little bright eyes	Small white dressmaker's eyes.
8. Collector of taxes	Tack hammer.
9. What a prizefighter expects	Sock on the nose (sock pinned on nose of a mask).
10. What young men often get	The mitten.
11. What every girl strives for	Beaus (a bunch of ribbon bows pinned to a card).
12. Famous Latin scholar	Cicero (a row of girls pasted on a card).
13. A paradise on earth	Two dice on a saucer of dirt.
14. A corncrib	Old shoe.
15. More holy than righteous	Old stocking full of holes.
16. A famous slipper	Banana peel.
17. What a baseball team must have	Pitcher.

Doublets

Home, School, Party   *Intermediates to Adults*

This contest provides fascinating diversion for those who like quiet play which calls for thinking. It is interesting either as competition in a group or as solitary amusement.

Two words are named of the same number of letters, these two words being called a "doublet." The contest consists of changing one word to the other by changing one letter at a time, each change making a standard word. That is, one letter in one of the words is changed, thus making a new word; then one letter of this word is changed to make still another word, and so on until the other half of the doublet is achieved.

The process becomes clear by studying an example: The doublet is "Pig and Sty." Changing one letter at a time, the words are as follows:

Pig — Pit — Pat — Pay — Say — Sty.

Other examples are as follows:

Hold — Hole — Hale — Have.
Fat — Fag — Fig — Pig.

Each intervening word is called a "link" and the contest is to see who can make the change with the fewest links.

Not all words can be linked together in this way, of course. Try the following:

Sad to Fun	Poor to Rich
Wet to Dry	Rest to Sofa
Pen to Ink	Black to White
Elm to Oak	Flour to Bread
Blue to Pink	Tears to Smile

Fill Ins

Party, Home   *Juniors to Adults*

The idea in this game is to fill in the missing letters to make four-letter words. The first and last letters are given, for example N — — T; by adding the letters E A we have *neat*.

Prepare cards with the first and last letters of a series of words such as the one given below. The left hand column usually spells some word—below, it spells "fill ins." Pass out the cards and have the players fill in the letters.

F	(O R)	K	I	(N C)	H
I	(R I)	S	N	(I C)	E
L	(A M)	P	S	(O A)	K
L	(O V)	E			

A Story of Songs

Party, Home, School   *Intermediates to Adults*

Divide the players into groups of four or five and seat each group at a table with paper and pencils. Give them ten minutes to compose a story using the titles of songs. Not more than two words may be used to connect the titles together.

Assemble the players and have the captain of each group read his story. Give a small prize for the best story.

For example, the story might start as follows:

When You and I Were Young, Maggie, we sat *Down by the Old Mill Stream In the Shade of the Old Apple Tree In the Blue Ridge Mountains of Virginia. In the Gloaming* the *Old Folks at Home* were *Comin' Thro' the Rye* with *Annie Laurie,* singing *Show Me the Way to Go Home, Sweet and Low. Old Black Joe* from *Dixie Land* waited by *The Old Spinning Wheel* holding *The Old Oaken Bucket.* . . .

Completing the Analogy

Party, School, Club, Home   *Juniors to Adults*

The players are seated in a compact group, and the leader reads an analogy such as "Father is to son as mother is to ————." The first player calling "Daughter" scores one point. The leader then reads others rapidly. The following list will prove suggestive of the type, and leaders can quickly compile a long list of others:

Father is to son as mother is to ———————— (daughter).
Foot is to shoe as hand is to ———————— (glove).
Dog is to pup as bear is to ———————— (cub).
Cow is to calf as deer is to ———————— (fawn).
Sheep is to lamb as frog is to ———————— (pollywog).
Hen is to chick as fish is to ———————— (minnow).
Hat is to head as coat is to ———————— (back).
Coat is to vest as shoe is to ———————— (sock).
Pencil is to paper as chalk is to ———————— (blackboard).
Balloon is to gas as football is to ———————— (air).
Scissors are to cloth as a razor is to ———————— (whiskers).
Sailboat is to sail as canoe is to ———————— (paddle).
Bow is to arrow as shotgun is to ———————— (shell).
Baseball is to bat as tennis ball is to ———————— (racket).
Pen is to ink as brush is to ———————— (paint).
Horse is to halter as dog is to ———————— (leash).

VARIATION.—Use such analogies as "Strong as an ———————— (ox)" or "Swift as a ———————— (deer)." The person completing the saying first scores one point. A list of over fifty such analogies will be found in Old Sayings, page 32.

High Brow Proverbs

Write proverbs on slips of paper and give one to each guest, then ask them to rewrite the proverbs in the most elegant language at their command.

For example, the proverb might be "Haste makes waste," and the high brow version might read, "An unwise accentuation of speed in performing a given task frequently results in an undesirable retardation in the rapidity with which the completion of the task is achieved, and a reduced output in the resultant commodities for which the task is performed."

Again, the proverb might be "People in glass houses shouldn't throw stones" and the revised version, "People who dwell in an abode constructed from the transparent, brittle, and fragile amorphous substance made by fusing together some form of silica should refrain from giving momentum to missiles of concreted earth or mineral matter."

A list of a hundred proverbs will be found on page 30.

Changing Proverbs

Ask each guest to write a proverb and after this is done, tell them to write a different saying following the typical style of proverbs which expresses the same idea as the proverb.

For example, the proverb "A new broom sweeps clean," might be rewritten to say "A worn broom lets the cobwebs gather." "You can't eat your cake and have it" might be expressed by saying "Pleasures enjoyed are pleasures spent."

Slang Tabooed

Give the players paper and pencil and ask them each to write a slang expression. When this is done, ask them to express the same thought in dignified language.

For example, one player might write as the slang expression "I'll bite." The dignified statement might read "I am willing to make myself the victim of your intended joke." Or, again, the slang expression might be "Blow me down," and the restatement, "I am so affected by what you say that you could remove me from my feet with a puff of your breath."

The Country Grocery Store

Parties, Home   *Juniors to Adults*

The players are seated in a circle. One begins by saying "I went to the country grocery store and bought some apples"; the next one says "I went to the country grocery store and bought some apples and beets"; the next one, "I went to the country grocery store and bought some apples, beets, and carrots"; and so on. Each player must "buy" some article in the country grocery store beginning with the next letter of the alphabet and repeat all articles purchased by those preceding him.

The idea is to run through the alphabet and see how many are still able to repeat the list and add new ones by the time the alphabet is completed and started over again. If a player omits an article, misnames one, mixes the alphabet, or is unable to call to mind an article for his letter in thirty seconds, he drops out of the game. Usually the circle is unable to go through the alphabet before all the players have missed.

Pack My Trunk for Klondike

Party, Club   *Juniors to Adults*

The players are seated in a circle. One starts by saying, "I packed my trunk for Klondike and I put in it a washrag." The next player says, "I packed my trunk for Klondike and I put in it a washrag and a shoe spoon." So the saying goes around the circle, each player repeating all the articles and adding one of his own. If any player forgets an article or names an article out of the sequence in which it was given, he becomes a half ghost as in Ghost or is made to pay a forfeit. (See Chapter X, "Forfeits for Social Gatherings.")

Music Box

Parties   *Juniors to Adults*

This is a test of the players' memory of music and their knowledge of popular tunes. Give each player a piece of paper and pencil. A pianist is necessary who can play many different tunes from memory. He should prepare beforehand a numbered list of the tunes and keep it before him. The tunes are played in medley fashion and each player attempts to write down the name of each as it is played. The tunes should consist of popular hits interspersed with old favorites. Give a small prize to the player who names the most tunes correctly.

Writing Love Letters

Divide the players in groups of from four to six, and seat them at a separate table. Provide each table with a couple of old magazines, writing paper, scissors, and paste.

Each group composes a love letter by clipping out phrases, sentences and words from the magazines and pasting them on writing paper. After about twenty minutes, the entire group is assembled and the letters read. Judges pick the best letter and a prize is given.

Prophecies

This event is particularly interesting when all know one another well. Place the names of each in a hat and have each guest draw one name out. Each writes a prophecy of the person whose name he drew, describing the person's situation fifteen years hence —business, family, health, education, and so on. After five or ten minutes, each reads the prophecy he wrote.

Who's Who.—The prophecy takes the form of a write-up in "Who's Who."

Illustrated Songs

Give each couple a paper and pencil and instruct them to draw a picture illustrating the name of a well-known song. The following are examples from a recent party: *The Old Spinning Wheel*— Father Time, a top with lines indicating that it is spinning, and a wheel; *Home, Sweet Home*—a house, a package with "Sugar" printed on it, and another house.

When finished, the drawings are numbered and hung on exhibition. Each player is provided with a card, and attempts to guess the names of the drawings and record them on the card opposite the number. The drawing wins which is guessed correctly by the largest number.

Editing the Corn Hollow Currier

This event may sound rather colorless but it is in fact a great fun-maker. Divide the group into a number of groups and seat each at a table with paper and pencils. Select a chief editor for each group and it might help if he were forewarned.

Assign to each group a department of the paper to edit, such as one of the following:

> City editor's department—local news.
> Political and national news.
> Foreign affairs.
> Society section.
> Sport section.
> Personal news.
> Betty Fairfax column.
> Fashions, beauty, household hints.
> Theatrical section.
> Editorials.

Each table prepares its section, dealing often with the personalities in the group as well as with a burlesque of the current news in general. After fifteen or twenty minutes, the group is assembled and the editor of each department reads his section for the entertainment of all.

Crambo Rhymes

Home, Party   *Intermediates to Adults*

Prepare beforehand a number of long slips of paper on which questions are written, and also an equal number of short slips on which words are written. These questions and words may be written beforehand and passed out, or the slips only may be prepared and passed out, asking each player to write a question on the long slip and a word on the short. Collect the slips and shake them up in a hat. Allow each player to draw one long slip and one short.

Each player must now prepare and recite a rhyme which answers the question and includes the word. For example, if the question were "When were you born?" and the word were "Bulldog," the rhyme might run:

> "In the month of May
> When the days were bright,
> My bulldog and I
> First saw the light."

Concealed Words

Party, Home, School   *Intermediates to Adults*

The object is to discover the words concealed in sentences. Give each a paper and pencil and dictate a proverb. Each player, working independently, writes all the words he can find in the sentence. All words must be made up of letters used in the *exact order* in which they appear in the sentence. No one-letter words are allowed.

Let us take for example the proverb "Barking dogs don't bite." The words concealed are as follows: bark, ark, kin, king, in, do, dog, don, on, bit, it.

This is individual play and is better suited to home and school than to parties.

Word Making

Party, School, Home   *Intermediates to Adults*

The hostess states a long word and tells each of the guests to write it at the top of a sheet of paper. It should be a word with many vowels. Then she gives ten minutes to see who can write the longest list of words, using only the letters found in the word and in no instance using any letter oftener than it appears in that word. It is a great deal easier to do this if the players group the words according to their initial letters.

Touching Up the Pictures

Party, Home   *Juniors to Adults*

Select a committee of three art judges—it adds to the fun to select them by chance. A number of pictures should be cut from magazines beforehand—portraits of people, prominent and otherwise. The movie magazines are full of ideal ones. Give each guest a picture and a heavy black pencil. Each guest touches up the pictures with eyebrows, mustaches, goatees, and so forth.

After ten minutes the guests sign their pictures and turn them in. They are pinned to the wall and the judges select the prize winners.

Spelling Bee

Parties, Social Gatherings   *Adults*

An old-fashioned spelling bee has excellent possibilities as a social contest for adults. The players take it in the spirit of fun and if the leader is clever in the selection of words, much merriment results.

FIFTY EASY WORDS

abscess	campaign	cyclone	hideous
aerial	cannibal	diagnose	honor
agility	casino	distill	irksome
arctic	charade	echo	juvenile
aisle	chocolate	eminent	kerosene
balloon	cocoa	foreign	knowledge
barren	concur	frolicking	linoleum
biceps	corps	gingham	masculine

moccasin
oar
operetta
pansy
pewter

professor
rabbit
religious
rescue
route

salmon
scallop
skillful
temperament
traveler

veranda
violin
weird

FIFTY MEDIUM–HARD WORDS

abbreviate
accessibility
acquiesce
amateur
anglicize
anonymous
asceticism
auxiliary
banister
battalion
bronchitis
catechism
cauliflower

chandelier
cognac
conundrum
decrepit
diocese
dudgeon
ecstasy
enumerator
epilogue
erasable
exemplary
fortieth
glycerine

guillotine
hollyhock
hyacinth
juiciness
languor
madonna
mischievous
mortgage
nasturtium
ostracize
penguin
piccolo
pleurisy

sacrilegious
sobriety
spittoon
stertorous
synopsis
trafficker
vaccinate
velocipede
veterinary
vitriol
witticism

FIFTY HARD WORDS

abysmal
alluvial
amoeba
anise
bazaar
blasphemy
bouillon
caisson
cantaloup
catarrh
catastrophe
charlatan
chrysanthemum

consanguinity
crystallize
emasculate
eschew
efficacious
formaldehyde
gaseous
hemorrhage
hydrangea
iridescence
isosceles
labyrinth
larghetto

liaison
llama
maelstrom
malfeasance
massacre
millennium
mnemonics
myrrh
parochial
promiscuity
pseudonym
pyrometer
reminiscence

riffraff
shibboleth
surcingle
therapeutics
ubiquitous
vacillation
venous
vicissitude
viviparous
xylophone
zephyr

Blind Pig

Parties   *Juniors to Adults*

Have the players sit around tables. Give each a paper and pencil. Put the lights out, ask all to close their eyes, and draw a blind pig on the paper. The pig must be complete except for the eyes which may be omitted since the pig is blind. When the lights come on, the laughs are sure to start. Each table selects its prize pig. The stunt may be played in the daylight by trusting the players to keep their eyes closed while they are making the drawings.

If the party is held near any seasonal holiday, substitute some appropriate object for the pig.

Tit-Tat-Toe

Home, Train, Automobile   *Juniors to Adults*

This ancient paper and pencil contest is still as intriguing as ever. Two players only can play the same game at once. Draw the lines on the paper illustrated in A, Figure 11. One player draws a circle in any one of the spaces and then the second player draws a cross

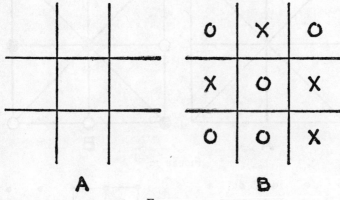

A   **B**

FIGURE 11

in any other space. They thus alternate in making their mark. The object is for a player to place three of his marks in a straight line, vertically, horizontally or diagonally. The player who made the circles in B won because he had three circles in a straight line, diagonally across the figure.

There is more to the contest than the uninitiated might suspect. The players alternate in starting. There are two systems of offense used which one will stumble onto in an evening or two of play. In general the player making the first mark has somewhat of an advantage and the strategy consists of throwing one's opponent on the defensive as soon as possible.

Square Tit-Tat-Toe

Home, Train, Automobile   *Juniors to Adults*

Draw on a paper the square and cross lines shown at A in Figure 12. Give one player five black buttons and the other five white ones. The players take turns in placing buttons on the intersections of the lines. The object is to place three buttons in a row, either straight across, up and down, or diagonally, and at the same time to prevent the other from doing this. The one succeeding in doing this wins.

In diagram B, the player with the black buttons wins because he has three buttons in a row.

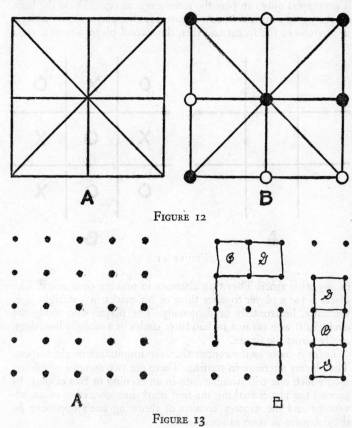

FIGURE 12

FIGURE 13

Closing Squares

Home, Train, Automobile   *Juniors to Adults*

This is another ancient contest which has withstood the test of time and probably will be popular for many years to come. It intrigues all ages until the late hours of the night.

Draw rows of dots on a paper as in A, Figure 13. Any number of dots may be used, but five in a row is customary.

Each player in turn draws a line connecting two dots, either vertically or horizontally. When a player succeeds in drawing the line that completes a square he puts his initial in the square, as illustrated in B. Whenever a player completes a square he has the privilege of drawing another line before his opponent takes his turn. The player wins who has the most initials in the squares when all squares are completed.

Forty-five Peg Puzzle

Home, Train   *Juniors to Adults*

Years of popularity give the best endorsement of the appeal of this puzzle.

To make the board, secure a piece of clear soft wood and bore or punch holes in it just large enough to insert match sticks in them.

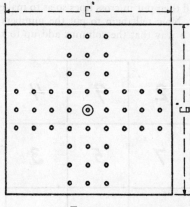

FIGURE 14

The design is illustrated in Figure 14. Break match sticks in two and insert one stick in each hole except the center one, which remains empty at the start.

The object is to remove all the pegs from the board by jumping them as in checkers and leave the last peg in the center hole.

The puzzle may be solved in forty-three moves.

THIRTY-THREE PEG PUZZLE.—The board is made as described above except it has thirty-three holes instead of forty-five. Leave off the outer row of three holes on each side of the diagram. This puzzle may be solved in thirty-one moves.

Five in a Row

Home, Train, Automobile   *Juniors to Adults*

A checkerboard and checkers are needed. Two players only may play at one time. Give one player the red checkers and the other the black ones.

Each player in turn places one checker on the board in any square he chooses. Each aims to get five of his checkers in a row, either vertically, horizontally, or diagonally. This requires careful study and holds a large element of interest. The player must not only try to form his own row but also take care to block the formation of his opponent's.

Fifteen

Home, Party   *Juniors to Adults*

Give each player paper and pencil and ask each to draw a square on the paper and then put in cross lines so as to make nine squares, as in Figure 15. Now tell them to put the numbers 1 to 9 in the squares in such a way that the columns add up to 15 in every di-

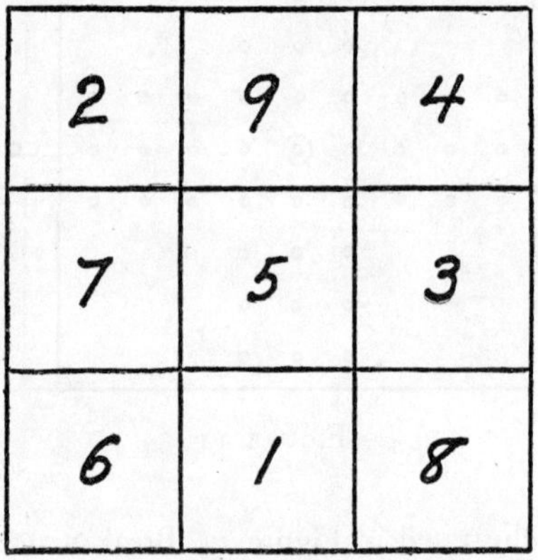

2	9	4
7	5	3
6	1	8

FIGURE 15

rection, vertically, horizontally, and diagonally. The one doing this first wins.

The method used in accomplishing this is to place 5 in the center square and 2, 4, 6, 8 in the four corner squares. The remaining numbers can be added with very little trouble. The diagram shows the completed squares.

Tricks with Numbers

Home, Party *Juniors to Adults*

There are many who particularly enjoy mathematical stunts involving the use of numbers. The following may be useful in planning for such groups.

GUESSING AGES, NUMBER 1.—This is a good trick by which to guess a person's age, but can of course be used with any number.

Ask the person to think of his age (or any number) and double it, add 1, multiply by 5, add 5, multiply by 10, and tell you the result. Subtract 100, strike off the last two digits, and the result will be the original number. Example:

Number selected	32
Double	64
Add 1	65
Multiply by 5	325
Add 5	330
Multiply by 10	3300
Subtract 100	3200
Strike off last two digits	32

GUESSING AGES, NUMBER 2.—Ask the person to think of his age (or any number), multiply it by 3, add 1, multiply by 3, add the original number, and tell you the result. Cross off the last digit, and the result is the original number. For example:

Number selected	27
Multiply by 3	81
Add 1	82
Multiply by 3	246
Add the original number	273
Strike off last digit	27

GUESSING AGES, NUMBER 3.—Ask each person to write down the number of the month in which he was born (2 for February), multiply it by 2, add 5, multiply by 50, add his age, subtract 365, add 115. The first digit or two digits will tell the month in which he was born and the last two digits will be his age.

Example:

Month (February)	2
Multiply by 2	4
Add 5	9
Multiply by 50	450
Add age (32)	482
Subtract 365	117
Add 115	232

He was born in February and is 32 years of age.

YOUR AGE AND YOUR MONEY.—Here's one that will tell you how old a person is and how much change he has in his pocket, all in one. Ask him to write down his age, multiply it by two, add five, and multiply by fifty. Now ask him to subtract 365, add to the result the amount of change he has in his pocket, and then add 115. Then ask him to tell you the result. The first two digits will be his age and the last two digits the amount of money he has.

Example:

Age	16
Multiplied by 2	32
Add 5	37
Multiply by 50	1850
Subtract 365	1485
Add change (12c)	1497
Add 115	1612

He is 16 years old and has 12c in his pocket.

NUMBER MAGIC.—This is one of the most interesting of the number tricks and never fails to make a hit, providing of course the group does not know the method. Write the number 1,089 on a slip of paper and ask one of the group to put it in his pocket without looking at it. Then ask him to write on a piece of paper any number of three digits that he chooses. Ask him to reverse the number and subtract the smaller from the larger. Then ask him to reverse the number which results and add it to the result. Now tell him to look at the slip in his pocket. His result will be 1,089.

Example:

Number chosen	842
Reversed	248
Subtracted	594
Reversed	495
Added	1,089

NAMING THE FIGURE.—Ask a person to think of a number and double it. Then give him an even number and tell him to add it on. Next tell him to divide the result by 2, and subtract the original number. Now you are able to tell him the exact remainder. It will be half the even number which you told him to add.

Number selected	20
Doubled	40
Even number added	12
Total	52
Divide by 2	26
Subtract original number	6

NINE.—Announce to the group that if they will take any number of three digits and subtract that number from the number reversed, you will tell them what the middle digit is. It will always be 9. For example, the number is 123—subtract it from 321, and the result is 198.

DIGITS.—Ask a person to write a number containing three digits, then reverse the number and subtract the smaller from the larger. Then ask him to tell you the last digit of his result, and you can tell him the whole number. When the numbers are reversed and subtracted the middle digit is always 9, and the first and last digits added together always make 9. You know to begin with that the middle digit is 9, and when he tells you the last digit you can find the first by subtracting the last from 9.

Example:

Number	843
Reversed	348
Result when subtracted	495

When he tells you the last digit is 5, subtract 5 from 9 and you know that the first digit is 4; consequently the number is 495.

Another example:

Number	201
Reversed	102
Result when subtracted	99

MENTAL MATHEMATICS.—Ask a person to write any number of three digits on a paper, then to reverse the number and subtract the smaller from the larger. To his surprise, you then tell him his result. You are able to do this by the following method: there are only nine possible answers: 99, 198, 297, 396, 495, 594, 693, 792, 891. As he subtracts, watch his pencil carefully from the other side of the room and you can detect the first figure he writes and that is all you need to know, provided you have memorized the above nine possible numbers.

ELEVEN.—Take any number less than 100, reverse it and add them. The resulting sum will always be divisible by 11. For example, the number is 27—add 72 and the sum is 99.

TRICK ADDING.—Ask the group to add four two's together so that the result will be five.

Solution: $2 + 2 + 2/2 = 5$

HIGHER MATHEMATICS.—If the number 12,345,679 is multiplied by any digit times 9 the result will contain nothing but the digit named. For example, $3 \times 9 = 27$. $12,345,679 \times 27 = 333,333,333$.

EASY MULTIPLICATION.—In multiplying a large number by 9, add 0 and subtract the original number from the new one—the result will be the same as if the original number had been multiplied by 9. Example: the number 147,672; add 0 and the number is 1,476,720. Subtract as follows:

$$
\begin{array}{r}
1,476,720 \\
-\ 147,672 \\
\hline
1,329,048
\end{array}
$$

$9 \times 147,672 = 1,329,048$

T Puzzle

Home, Party   *All Ages*

This appears to be a very simple puzzle, yet it is confusing and difficult even to those who have solved it several times before.

Cut out a letter T of the dimensions in the diagram and cut it into the four sections indicated by the dotted lines. The puzzle consists of fitting the pieces together into the letter T.

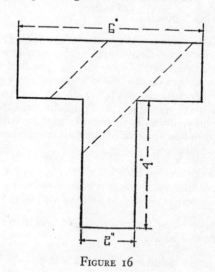

FIGURE 16

F Puzzle

Home, Club   *Juniors to Adults*

Draw a letter F on a cardboard and cut it into pieces as indicated in the drawing. Shuffle the pieces and put them together into a letter F again.

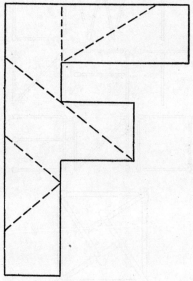

Figure 17

Match Tricks

Party, Home   *Juniors, Intermediates*

Match tricks hold a peculiar appeal to many. There are many of these, of which the following are examples.

Two.—Form three squares with twelve matches. Take away any two and leave two. (Figure 18.)

Ten.—Form three squares with twelve matches. Take away three and leave ten. (Figure 18.)

One.—Form three squares with twelve matches. Take any one and leave one. (Figure 18.)

Squares and Triangles.—Using eight matches, form two squares and four triangles. (Figure 18.)

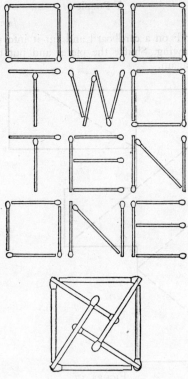

FIGURE 18

Coin Tricks

Party, Home   *Juniors, Intermediates*

TRICK NUMBER 1.—Arrange six coins in the form of a right angle as in Figure 19. Move one coin and have two rows of four coins each. Solution: Place the lower coin on top of the corner coin.

TRICK NUMBER 2.—Arrange six coins in the form of a cross as in Figure 19. Move one coin and have two rows of four coins. Solution: Place the lower coin on top of the center coin.

Brain Twisters

Sisters and brothers have I none but that man's father (looking at a portrait) is my father's son. *Answer:* Portrait of his son.

When a woman was asked how many ducks she had, she replied,

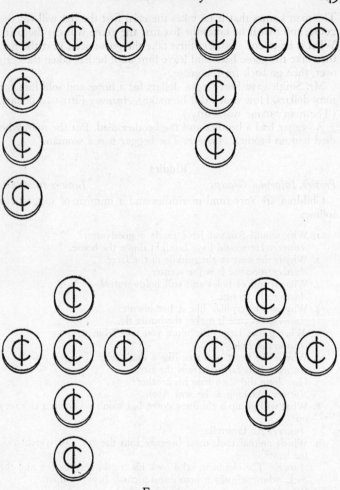

FIGURE 19

"As they all ran down the path I saw there was a duck in front of two ducks, a duck behind two ducks, and a duck between two ducks. How many ducks were there?" *Answer:* Three ducks, one after the other.

A man with some corn, a fox, and a goose finds it necessary to cross a river and he is not willing to leave any of these possessions behind and yet his boat is only large enough to carry one at a time.

The man knows that if he takes the corn first the fox will eat the goose, and that if he takes the fox first the goose will eat the corn. What is he to do? *Answer:* First take the goose over, next the fox, then take the goose back and leave him until he has taken the corn over, then go back for the goose.

Mr. Smith gave Forty eight dollars for a horse and sold him for sixty dollars. How much did he make? *Answer:* Fifty-two dollars. (The man's name was Forty.)

A beggar had a brother and the brother died. But the man who died had no brother. *Answer:* The beggar was a woman.

Riddles

Parties, Informal Groups   *Juniors to Adults*

Children are very fond of riddles and a number of suggestions follow:

1. Why would Samson have made a good actor?
   Answer: He would have brought down the house.
2. Why is the nose in the middle of the face?
   Answer: Because it is the scenter.
3. What is full of holes and still holds water?
   Answer: A sponge.
4. Why is a caterpillar like a hot biscuit?
   Answer: Because it makes the butter fly.
5. What grows larger the more you take from it?
   Answer: A hole.
6. Why is the heart of a tree like a dog's tail?
   Answer: It is farthest from the bark.
7. How long did Cain hate his brother?
   Answer: As long as he was Abel.
8. What will go up a chimney down but won't go down a chimney up?
   Answer: An umbrella.
9. Which animal took most luggage into the ark and which took the least?
   Answer: The elephant, who took his trunk, and the fox and the cock, who had only a brush and a comb between them.
10. Why is an orange like a church belfry?
    Answer: Because you usually get a peel (peal) from it.
11. Why does a horse eat in an odd way?
    Answer: Because he eats best when he hasn't a bit in his mouth.
12. When is a doctor most annoyed?
    Answer: When he is out of patients.
13. When did George Washington first ride in a four-wheeled vehicle?
    Answer: When he took his first hack at the cherry tree.
14. At what time of the day was Adam created?
    Answer: A little before Eve.

15. What is the difference between a garden hose and a Chinaman?
    Answer: One keeps the lawn wet and the other keeps the lawn dry (laundry).
16. What is the difference between an old penny and a new dime?
    Answer: Nine cents.
17. Why are fish considered well educated?
    Answer: Because they are generally found in schools.
18. Why is Ireland apt to become the wealthiest country in the world?
    Answer: Because its capital is always Dublin (doublin').
19. What table has no legs to stand on?
    Answer: The multiplication table.
20. What is the difference between one yard and two yards?
    Answer: Usually a fence.
21. What colors would you paint the sun and the wind?
    Answer: The sun rose and the wind blue (blew).
22. Why should you never tell secrets in a corn field?
    Answer: Because corn has ears and is bound to be shocked.
23. What is the difference between a cat and a comma?
    Answer: A cat has its claws at the end of its paws, and a comma its pause at the end of its clause.
24. When was money first mentioned in the Bible?
    Answer: When the dove brought the green back to Noah.
25. How are lollypops like race horses?
    Answer: Because the more you lick them the faster they go.
26. When a boy falls in water what is the first thing he does?
    Answer: Gets wet.
27. What would happen if a man should swallow his teaspoon?
    Answer: He wouldn't be able to stir.
28. Why is life the greatest of all conundrums?
    Answer: Because we all have to give it up.
29. What is it from which you may take away the whole and still have some left?
    Answer: The word "wholesome."
30. If a two-wheeled wagon is a bicycle, and a three-wheeled wagon a tricycle, what is a five-wheeled wagon?
    Answer: A V-hicle.
31. Why does a freight train need no locomotive?
    Answer: Because the freight will make a cargo (car go).
32. When is money damp?
    Answer: When it's due (dew) in the morning and it's missed (mist) at night.
33. When did Moses sleep five in a bed?
    Answer: When he slept with his forefathers.
34. Who are the two largest ladies in the United States?
    Answer: Miss Ouri and Mrs. Sippi.
35. What is the difference between a cloud and a whipped boy?
    Answer: One pours with rain and the other roars with pain.
36. What is the difference between a watchmaker and a jailer?
    Answer: One sells watches and the other watches cells.

37. What is the difference between a fisherman and a lazy schoolboy?
    Answer: One baits his hook and the other hates his book.

38. What is the difference between a man going upstairs and a man looking upstairs?
    Answer: One is stepping up the stairs and the other staring up the steps.

39. What is filled every morning and emptied every night, except once a year when it is filled at night and emptied in the morning?
    Answer: A stocking.

40. What is the keynote of good manners?
    Answer: B natural.

41. What kind of a noise annoys an oyster?
    Answer: A noisy noise annoys an oyster.

42. What is it that goes from New York to Albany without moving?
    Answer: The road.

43. Why is a dog biting his tail a good manager?
    Answer: Because he makes both ends meet.

44. Why wasn't the Statue of Liberty placed on Brooklyn Bridge?
    Answer: Because she liked her bed low. (Bedloe Island.)

45. Who is the first man mentioned in the Bible?
    Answer: Chap one. (Chap. I.)

46. Which is the longest word in the English language?
    Answer: Smiles. It has a mile between the first and last letters.

47. Why is U the jolliest letter?
    Answer: Because it is always in the midst of fun.

48. What sea might be used for a bedroom if the house were crowded?
    Answer: Adriatic. (A dry attic.)

49. There was a girl in our town,
    Silk an' satin was her gown,
    Silk an' satin, gold an' velvet
    Guess her name, three times I've tell'd it.
    Answer: Anne.

50. Sometimes I am very sly;
    Other times a trade I ply;
    Over the billows swift I fly;
    Now, pray tell me, what am I?
    Answer: Craft.

51. Why are weary people like automobile wheels?
    Answer: Because they are tired.

TRADE RIDDLES.—

1. What trade is it whose best works are trampled upon?
   Answer: Shoemaker.

2. What trade does the sun follow?
   Answer: Tanner.

3. What trade does the president follow?
   Answer: Cabinet maker.

4. Of what trade can it be said that all its members are men of letters?

Answer: Printer.

5. Of what trade is a little tin dog?
   Answer: Tinker (tin-cur).
6. Of what trade is the preacher at a wedding?
   Answer: Joiner.
7. Of what trade is the sun in May?
   Answer: Mason (May-sun).
8. What trade is best qualified to cook a hare?
   Answer: Hairdresser.
9. What trade is noted among the authors of English literature?
   Answer: Goldsmith.

Nut Riddles.—

1. What nut is spread on biscuits and griddle cakes?
   Answer: Butternut.
2. What nut is a picture hung on?
   Answer: Walnut.
3. What nut grows under the ground?
   Answer: Peanut.
4. What nut is used for a trunk?
   Answer: Chestnut.
5. What nut borders the sea?
   Answer: Beechnut.
6. What nut do people drink?
   Answer: Cocoanut.
7. What nut makes a noise like a sneeze?
   Answer: Cashew nut.

Tongue Twisters

1. She sells sea shells by the seashore.
2. Three gay geese on three green hills.
   Gray were the geese and green were the hills.
3. Peter Piper picked a peck of pickled peppers;
   A peck of pickled peppers Peter Piper picked.
   If Peter Piper picked a peck of pickled peppers,
   Where is the peck of pickled peppers Peter Piper picked?
4. "Amidst the mists with angry boasts
   He thrusts his fists against the posts
   And still insists he sees the ghosts."
5. Sarah sits by six sick city slickers.
6. Three throbbing thumping thrush thoroughly thwarting thirty thrashers.
7. Round the rough and rugged rock the ragged rascal rudely ran.
8. How much wood would a woodchuck chuck
   If a woodchuck would chuck wood?
9. Nine nimble noblemen nibbling nuts.
10. Eve eating eagerly elegant Easter eggs.
11. "Robert Rowley rolled a round ball round."

12. One obstinate old ostrich ordering ordinary oranges.
13. Fresh flesh of fresh fried fish.
14. Four fat friars fanning flickering flames.
15. Sister Susie's swiftly sewing sixty shirts for soldiers.
16. Seven serious southern soldiers setting sail south suddenly.
17. Two tiny timid toads trying to trot to Tarrytown.
18. Ten tiny titmice tipping ten tall tamarack trees.
19. Sarah in a shawl shoveled soft snow softly.
20. Six thick thistle sticks.
21. She is a thistle sifter. She has a sieve of sifted thistles and a sieve of unsifted thistles, for she is a thistle sifter.
22. Quizzical Quiz, kiss me quick.
23. "David Daldrom dreamt he drove a dragon.
    Did David Daldrom dream he drove a dragon?
    If David Daldrom dreamt he drove a dragon,
    Where's the dragon David Daldrom dreamt he drove?"
24. "Oliver Ogilvie ogled an olive and oyster.
    Did Oliver Ogilvie ogle an olive and oyster?
    If Oliver Ogilvie ogled an olive and oyster,
    Where is the olive and oyster Oliver Ogilvie ogled?"
25. Theophilus Thistle thrust three thousand thistles through the thick of his thumb.

Where Letters Are Equal to Words

Parties   *Juniors to Adults*

The guests are asked to answer certain questions by using letters of the alphabet. Below are the questions and the answers:

What letter is a human organ?	I
What letter is a beverage?	T
What letter is a bird?	J
What letter is a vegetable?	P
What letter is an insect?	B
What letter is a clew?	Q
What letter is a part of a house?	L
What letter is a large body of water?	C
What letter is a sheep?	U
What letter is a command to oxen?	G
What letter is a verb of debt?	O
What 2 letters are the condition of a winter pavement?	I-C
What 2 letters name a county in England?	S-X
What 2 letters make a word meaning too much?	X-S
What 2 letters name a creeping vine?	I-V
What 2 letters name a verb that means to rot or fall in ruins?	D-K
What 2 letters name a word meaning not difficult?	E-Z
What 2 letters name a girl's name?	K-T
What 2 letters name a written composition?	S-A
What 2 letters name a summer dress goods?	P-K

What 2 letters name a kind of pepper? .... K-N
What 2 letters name a word meaning to surpass others? .... X-L
What 2 letters name a word resembling jealousy? .... N-V

Famous People of Story Land [1]

Parties   *Juniors to Adults*

1. Who lived a long time all alone on an island? Robinson Crusoe.
2. Who lost her slipper? Cinderella.
3. Who found the cave of the forty thieves? Ali Baba.
4. Who stole the singing harp? Jack the Giant Killer.
5. Who cut off her hair to help her mother? Jo in "Little Women."
6. Who fell down and bumped his crown? Jill's brother, Jack.
7. Who stole a pig? Tom, the Piper's Son.
8. Who had a blackbird pie for his dinner? The King.
9. Who said "Off with her head"? The Duchess in "Alice in Wonderland."
10. Who had a playmate named Minnehaha? Hiawatha.
11. Who liked to smoke and listen to his fiddlers? Old King Cole.
12. Who asked the crocodile what he liked to eat? Baby Elephant in Kipling's "Just So" stories.
13. Who fell off the wall? Humpty Dumpty.
14. Who had a wonderful wishing lamp? Aladdin.
15. Who took a twenty-year nap on a hillside? Rip Van Winkle.
16. Who lost their mittens? The Three Little Kittens.
17. Who could eat no fat? Jack Spratt.
18. Who went a wooing? The Froggy.
19. When do dogs bark? When the Beggars come to town.
20. Who put the pussy cat in the Well? Little Tommy Green.
21. Who lost her sheep? Little Bo-Peep.
22. Who went to sleep in the haystack? Little Boy Blue.
23. Who ran up the clock? The Mouse.
24. Who lived in the shoe? The old woman.
25. Who put the kettle on? Polly.

About the United States

Parties   *Juniors to Adults*

The guests are told to answer on paper the following questions by writing the abbreviations of states in the United States. The players do not write the questions, but just give the answers, numbering each. Here are the questions with the answers:

1. Which state is the cleanest? .... Wash.
2. Which state is the most religious? .... Mass.
3. Which state never forgets itself? .... Me.

[1] From B. T. Hayhow, "The 'Party-a-Month'—Merry Christmas and a Happy New Year," *Pentathlon,* December, 1929.

4. Which state saved Noah and his family? .... Ark.
5. Which state is a physician? .... Md.
6. Which state is a grain? .... R. I.
7. Which state seems to be in poor health? .... Ill.
8. Which state is an exclamation? .... O.
9. Which state is a parent? .... Pa.
10. Which state is to cut long grass? .... Mo.
11. Which state is to study carefully? .... Conn.
12. Which state is a number? .... Tenn.
13. Which state is metal in its natural formation? .... Ore.
14. Which state is the happiest? .... Ga.

Penny Wise

Parties   *Juniors to Adults*

Each player is provided with a Lincoln penny, and paper and pencil. On the paper beforehand or to dictation are written the following items, without the answers, of course.

The player who has the largest number of correct answers keeps his penny. The answers must be found on the penny:

> The name of a song. (America)
> A privilege. (Liberty)
> A small animal. (Hare) (hair)
> A part of Indian corn. (Ear)
> A part of a hill. (Brow)
> Something denoting self. (Eye) (I)
> Part of a door. (Lock) (of hair)
> A foreign fruit. (Date)
> What ships sail on. (Sea) (C)
> A perfume. (Scent) (Cent)
> A Chinese beverage. (Tea) (T)
> A term of marriage. (United States)
> Part of a plant. (Leaf)
> A religious edifice. (Temple)
> A messenger. (One sent) (Cent)
> A method of voting. (Ayes and noes) (Eyes and nose)

CHAPTER VIII

SMALL EQUIPMENT GAMES FOR CLUB ROOM AND HOME

A CLUB or organization need not want for play equipment for its club room or play room, even though it does not have the funds to purchase the elaborate equipment frequently found in club rooms. Simple homemade equipment, costing little but the time it takes to make it, can be provided, which will bring all the joy that high-priced game gadgets will.

"Fun not bought with money" is an excellent recreation maxim, and it applies to club-room equipment as well as to commercialized recreation. A game that is simplicity itself and costs but a half-hour of time for the making may prove as challenging to club members as an elaborate item costing hundreds of dollars.

This chapter suggests a few such articles of club-room game equipment which cost little or nothing, but which have proven very satisfactory.

Box Hockey

Home, Club, Party, Picnic   *Juniors to Adults*

This is a very popular game, and since it can be played strenuously in a small room and without damage to furniture, it is ideal for home use. As a game for small club rooms it has few equals in adaptability and popularity.

Equipment.—The frame illustrated in the diagram must be built. It consists of sides, ends, and a middle partition, but has no bottom. It is made out of two-inch lumber. While it may be eight, ten, or twelve feet long, a length of ten feet is recommended for average conditions. Each end board has a hole cut at the bottom in semicircular form as illustrated in Figure 20, three and one-half inches wide. The middle partition has two such holes at the bottom and a groove cut in the center of the top two inches wide.

An old baseball and two flat, boy's hockey sticks are needed.

The Play.—Two players only can play at a time. They stand on opposite sides of the box, facing it. Each player's goal is the hole at the end of the box to his left. The object is to hit the ball through this hole with the hockey stick.

At the start the ball is placed in the groove at the top of the middle partition. The two players place their hockey sticks on the floor on opposite sides of the partition, raise them and strike them together above the ball; this is done three times and after the

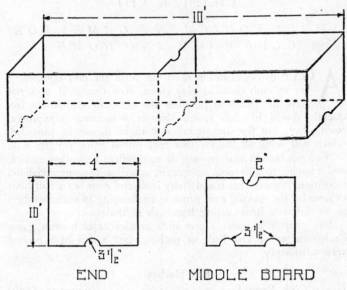

END   MIDDLE BOARD

FIGURE 20

third tap they attempt to hit the ball. If the ball falls into the half of the box to the player's right he must work it through the holes in the partition into the section to his left, and then he is in position to attempt to score. If the ball is knocked out of the box it is put in play by placing it on the floor in the box opposite the point where it went out, and the players tap their sticks above it three times as at the start.

Scoring.—One point is scored each time a player puts the ball through the hole in the end of the box to his left. Five points constitute a game.

Parlor Polo

Club, Home   *Juniors to Adults*

This interesting little table game calls for a box made exactly like that shown above in Figure 20 for Box Hockey, except that it is made on a miniature scale. The box is made of quarter-inch stuff and is twenty-four inches long, twelve inches wide, and four inches high. Like the box-hockey box, it has no bottom, but is set on a table. A marble is used for a ball and lead pencils for sticks. The game is played exactly as in Box Hockey.

Dart Throwing

Club, Home, Playground, Camp   *Juniors to Adults*

Dart throwing is one of the most universally fascinating of the club-room and summer-camp activities.

Excellent darts can be purchased very inexpensively. For club-room use, a piece of wall board five feet square may be used for the target board. Paint a target on it consisting of ten concentric circles. The bull's-eye is three inches in diameter and each succeeding circle one and one-half inches from the next smaller. Thus the target is thirty inches wide, and when placed on the five-foot board, there is plenty of board outside the target to stop poorly-aimed darts. Number the circles from the center out, 10 to 1. The board should be nailed on two uprights and set up against the wall. Establish a throwing line fifteen to twenty feet distant.

For outdoor use, a board six feet square should be used, with a target five feet wide painted on it.

Each player throws one dart each turn. Each dart scores in the circle in which it sticks. Those on a line score in the higher circle. There are two ways to score: (1) the player wins who scores one hundred first; (2) the player wins who has the highest score when all have thrown thirty-six (eighteen) darts.

There is an element of danger in dart throwing and the play needs careful supervision when children are participating. All should be kept behind the throwing line until all the darts have been thrown; then all go to the board to recover the darts.

Rope Quoits

Parties, Home, Club   *Juniors to Adults*

The equipment for this indoor form of quoits can easily be made at home. In the center of a piece of board eight inches square and one inch thick, bore a one-inch hole; in this hole insert a section of a broomstick or similar peg so that it sits up to a height of five inches. The quoits may be made of rope or rubber hose. The rope quoits are six inches in diameter, outside dimensions, and may be more quickly made as follows: Cut a five-foot section of one-fourth inch rope and make a five-inch coil in the center; then twist the ends tightly around and around the loop; tuck the ends under and hold them by wrapping them tightly with adhesive tape. The hose quoits are made from fourteen inches of old rubber hose; coil the hose into a circle and hold by wrapping securely with adhesive tape. Two pegs and four quoits are needed.

Place the pegs from twelve to fifteen feet apart and play according to the regular rules of Quoits.

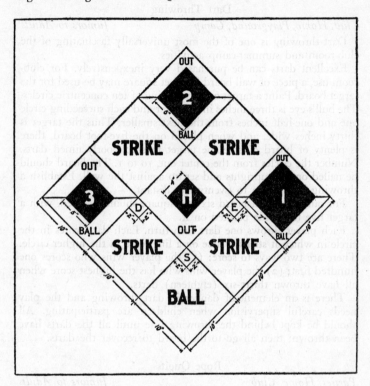

FIGURE 21

Dart Baseball

Club, Home, Playground, Camp   *Juniors to Adults*

Paint the diagram shown in Figure 21 on a board or piece of wall board five feet square. If desired, this design may be painted on the back of the bull's-eye target board described above in Dart Throwing. By turning the board around, either type of contest may thus be played.

The throwing line should be fifteen feet distant. The players choose sides. One team is "at bat" and throws until it is out; then the other side throws. Square "H" is a home run, "1" is a single, "2" is a two-base hit, and "3" a three-base hit. When a player makes a hit, he leaves the dart in the square and advances if the following player hits. If the batter hits "E" (error) or "D" (dead ball) he takes his base. "S" stands for a sacrifice hit. If a dart fails to stick in the board and falls, or does not hit the board, the batter is out.

Ring Golf

Club, Home, Picnic   *Juniors to Adults*

Make nine pegs as described in Ring Quoits and station them at various points around the room. Part of them may be in one room and part in another. If outdoors, drive broomsticks painted white in the ground at intervals of 100 to 150 feet. Each player needs a rope or rubber-hose quoit made as described in Ring Quoits.

The players throw in turn for the first peg, counting the throws required to ring it. Each throw is made from the point where the preceding throw came to rest. The player wins who completes the nine pegs in the fewest throws.

Bull-Board

Home, Party, Club   *Juniors to Adults*

This is a popular ship-board game which may be played anywhere. It requires but a small space and the equipment is simple and easily made.

The bull-board diagram illustrated in Figure 22 may be drawn or painted on the floor, but it is much more satisfactory to prepare a board for the purpose. The board is three by four feet in size, made out of one-inch lumber. Under the top edge nail a four-inch board so that when the board is laid on the floor it has a slight slope toward the players. Paint the design on it, making each square twelve inches. Number the squares as illustrated.

Ten disks of wood are needed. They are four inches in diameter and sawed out of half-inch lumber. The sides of the disks may be covered with canvas glued to the wood. Half of the disks should be painted one color and half another color.

Place the bull-board on the floor and establish a throwing line twelve to fifteen feet distant. The distance should suit the ability of the players.

The game is played between two players. Each has five disks and they take turns in throwing them at the board. When all are

thrown, the inning is over and the score counted. Each disk scores
the number of the square in which it rests at the end of the inning.
Those touching division lines score in the higher square. If a disk
touches a "bull" square, the player loses all of the points made that
inning. However if both bull squares are touched by his disks they

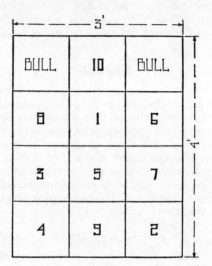

FIGURE 22

cancel each other. The disks do not count in the squares where
they land when thrown, but where they are at the end of the
inning.

If a player steps over the line in throwing, the disk is dead for
the inning and is removed at once.

The player wins who scores one hundred points first.

SEQUENCE BULL-BOARD.—This is the type of game most frequently played on a bull-board but it is more difficult and usually
not as interesting to beginners as the above.

The object is to throw the disks so that they land in the squares
in the following order:

> Squares 1 to 10 consecutively
> The right-hand bull square
> The left-hand bull square
> The left-hand bull square
> The right-hand bull square
> Squares 10 to 1 consecutively

A player continues to throw for a square until he makes it. When the inning is over, he takes up his play on his next turn by throwing for the square next higher than the last one he made.

All the disks are left on the board until the player completes his five throws. Disks touching a division line do not count but may be knocked into the desired area by succeeding disks.

If a disk rests in one of the "bull" squares out of its proper order, the player must start over again, beginning with one if going up, or ten if going down. If a disk falls off the board the player is set back one square; that is, if he were playing for the 3 square, he would have to play for the 2 square.

The player wins who first completes the circuit of the squares in their designated order.

PENNY BULL-BOARD.—This is a simple variation of Bull-Board which is particularly interesting for home play or for rotative parties. Draw the bull-board diagram (Figure 22) on the floor with chalk next to a wall. Each square should be five inches in size. Establish a throwing line six feet distant.

Each player tosses five pennies, one after another. He adds up the total of the squares in which his pennies rest to obtain his score. Pennies resting on a line score in the higher square. If a penny comes to rest in a bull square, all pennies thrown previously do not count and the player is entitled only to the score made on the following throws.

After all have thrown, the one with the highest score wins.

Exo

Club, Home *Juniors to Adults*

In his excellent book *Homemade Games* [1] Arthur H. Lawson describes the following variation of Bull-board. A more detailed description can be found in *Homemade Games*.

The board is exactly like the board used in Bull-board (see Figure 22) except that there is an additional row of squares across the bottom which is an exact duplicate of the top row. In place of the word "Bull" the letter X is used. Thus both the top and bottom rows of squares read

X   10   X

The disks are the same as in Bull-board.

If a board is made for Exo, it can be used for both Exo and Bull-board. In playing Bull-board, just disregard the bottom row of squares.

[1] Arthur H. Lawson, *Homemade Games,* p. 127. Philadelphia: J. B. Lippincott Company, 1934.

The game is played between two players. The players take turns in throwing their disks at the board. Each has five disks. When all are thrown, the inning is over, and the disks are retrieved. If a player steps over the throwing line, the disk is dead and counts for nothing.

Each disk scores the number of the square on which it rests when the player's turn is completed, and the score is added. A disk touching a division line scores in the higher square. If a disk touches an X square, the player loses all points scored that inning. However, if two X's are touched in one inning, they cancel each other. If a player scores three X's in an inning, his score for that inning is doubled. If he scores four X's, his total score is doubled.

The player wins who scores one hundred points first.

Sequence Exo.—This game requires considerably more skill than Exo. The object is to toss the disks so that they will score in the following order:

> 1 to 10 consecutively
> Upper Right X
> Upper Left X
> Lower Left X
> Lower Right X
> 10 to 1 consecutively

If an X is thrown out of order in an inning, the player loses one point; that is, if the last square he made going up is 5, he must play for 5 over again. If he throws two X's in one inning, they cancel each other. If he scores three X's he must start over again, or go back to 10 if he is going down. If he makes all four X's they cancel each other.

Fruit Jar Ring Toss

Home, Party, Club   *Juniors to Adults*

Into a board twenty-four by eighteen inches, nails are driven and numbered as in Figure 23. The nails should extend out from the board at least two and one-half inches and should be tilted at a slight angle upward. The board is hung on a wall. For a permanent board for a clubroom, round-headed screws may be used instead of nails and the board varnished. The throwing line is about nine or ten feet distant. Ordinary large-sized can rubbers or fruit-jar rings are used.

The contestants take turns in throwing, each throwing three rings each turn. Each ring scores the number marked under the nail on which it hangs. Twenty-one points constitute the game.

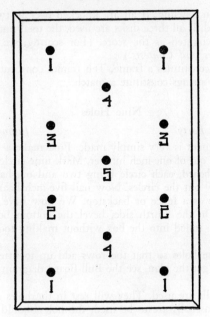

FIGURE 23

Skittles

Club, Playground, Camp, Yard   *Juniors to Adults*

This excellent little game of the tenpin type, taken from *Homemade Games* [2] is more satisfactory than Tenpins in that it does not require a smooth floor. Instead of using a ball, a disk is used.

If small tenpins are available, use them. Otherwise, use ten round sticks three inches in diameter and nine inches long. Set them up in the triangular form used in Tenpins with the apex toward the bowling line. The disks are of wood, four and a half inches wide and one and one-quarter to one and one-half inches thick. Twelve disks are needed.

The disks are propelled in two ways: one may slide them if the floor is smooth enough, or if outdoors, they may be thrown with the flat toss as in Horseshoe Pitching.

The players take turns in throwing. Each is entitled to three throws each turn. If all pins are knocked over by one disk, a strike

[2] Arthur H. Lawson, *Homemade Games,* p. 74. Philadelphia: J. B. Lippincott Company, 1934.

is scored as in bowling. If all are knocked over in two throws, a spare is scored. If all three disks are used, the total number of pins displaced is counted as the score. (For scoring, see Bowling in *Active Games and Contests*.)

Each turn constitutes a frame. Ten frames constitute a game or string. Three strings constitute a match.

Nine Holes [3]

Club, Home, Party   *Juniors to Adults*

The equipment is very simply made. First make a board thirty inches square out of one-inch lumber. Mark nine circles, three in a row, on the board, each circle being two and one-half inches in diameter. Saw out the circles. Now nail five-inch boards on three sides to serve as a fence or backstop. We now have a box with three sides. On the fourth side, bevel the bottom board so that a ball may be rolled into the box without making too much of a bounce.

Number the holes so that the rows add up to fifteen in every direction. To get the plan, see the Bull-Board diagram (Figure 22, page 162).

Croquet balls are used. They will rest in the holes and not fall through. If baseballs are to be used, the holes should be smaller.

Place the board on the floor and elevate the back side of it five inches by placing a block of wood or some books under it. Fifteen feet from the open side, draw a throwing line.

The game is best played by two players. Each has three balls, and they alternate in rolling. When all six balls have been rolled, the inning is over. Each player scores the number of the holes where his balls rest when the inning is over. If a ball comes to rest in a hole and a subsequent ball displaces it, it does not count unless of course it stops in another hole.

A ball is dead and is removed at once if the player threw the ball instead of rolling it, or stepped over the line in bowling.

The player wins who first scores one hundred points.

SEQUENCE NINE HOLES.—The object is to score in the holes in the following order: 1 to 9 consecutively, and 9 to 1 consecutively. The balls count as they rest at the end of the inning. If at the end of the first inning a player has balls resting in holes 1 and 2, he will throw for hole 3 at the start of the next inning. The player wins who completes the routine first.

[3] Arthur H. Lawson, *Homemade Games,* p. 137. Philadelphia: J. B. Lippincott Company, 1934.

Washer Baseball

Parties, Home, Sidewalk, Club   *Juniors to Adults*

The diagram illustrated in Figure 24 is marked out with chalk on the floor or sidewalk. The throwing line is ten to twelve feet distant. Purchase from the hardware store a dozen washers, four inches in diameter or as large as can be obtained.

The group divides into two teams, one at bat and the other in the field. The team in the field does nothing but return the

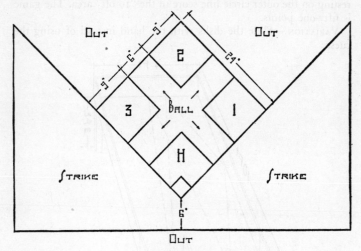

FIGURE 24

washers. The first batter takes his position at the throwing line and throws or slides washers at the diagram until he is out by striking out or flying out to the field, or until he gets on base by a hit or four balls. The regular routine of baseball is followed. The batting side continues at bat until it has three outs, then the teams reverse positions.

Target Shuffle

Club, Party   *Juniors to Adults*

With chalk or paint mark a fifteen-inch square on the floor or near one end of a table-tennis table. In it draw four concentric circles, the inner one four inches in diameter and the others four inches from the next smaller. Number the circles 10, 5, 3, and 1.

The areas in the square outside the outer circle are marked "10 off."

The disks are cut from three-fourths-inch wood and are two and one-half inches in diameter. The cues are made from the same pattern used in making regular shuffleboard cues, but are only thirty inches long over all; the shovel part is four inches long. (See Shuffleboard in *Active Games and Contests*.)

Establish a serving line eight feet away and play as in Shuffleboard. Disks resting on a line score in the higher circle. Those resting on the outer circle line score in the "10 off" area. The game is fifty-one points.

VARIATION.—Slide the disks with the hand instead of using the cues.

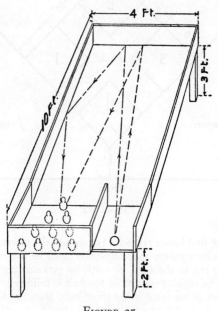

FIGURE 25

Table Bowling

Club Room, Home   *Juniors, Intermediates*

The table is a box-like structure on legs, built as illustrated in Figure 25. It is ten feet long and four feet wide. A set of tenpins is needed, obtainable from a toy store. Ordinary hard baseballs are used.

The tenpins are placed in the position on the board illustrated in the diagram. The player rolls the ball from the opening at the lower end so that it hits the board at the upper end, rebounds, and knocks down the tenpins. Each player has two bowls each frame unless he knocks all the pins down with one bowl. The scoring is as in Bowling (see *Active Games and Contests*). Knocking all the pins down with one bowl counts a strike, all in two bowls, a spare. The game is ten frames as in Bowling.

Disk Croquet [4]

Club, Home   *Juniors to Adults*

This is an indoor game of Croquet, and as the name implies, is played with a disk instead of a ball. It can be played in any room twenty by thirty feet in size, or smaller if necessary.

The disks are about three inches wide and one inch thick. Regular croquet mallets are used. The wickets are of wire, each end of which is stuck into a small block of wood so that it will stand on the floor. The wicket should be six inches high and three and three-fourths inches wide.

Arrange the wickets as in regular Croquet, using whatever space is available. For stakes, a spot may be marked on the floor, or a two-inch stick may be set up.

The game follows the regular rules of Croquet, but it will be found that the game calls for skills all its own.

Skully
(*Chinese Checkers*)

Playground, Home, Club, Party   *Juniors to Adults*

Skully is an old game of the city streets, but since it requires a space only three feet square, and equipment that can be found easily, it is excellent as a game for the home.

Court.—Outdoors, the court is laid out on a square of a concrete sidewalk, three by three feet. Indoors, the top of a card table is ideal, or a square may be drawn on the floor. Lay out the court with chalk as illustrated in Figure 26. The squares are four inches square and numbered as illustrated. The rectangle in the center measures eight by twelve inches and has diagonal lines connecting the corners. This rectangle is known as the "pit." Bases Number 9 and Number 10 adjoin it on either side.

[4] The idea for this game was taken from A. H. Lawson, *Homemade Games*, p. 85. Copyright 1934. By permission of J. B. Lippincott Company, publishers.

Equipment.—Each player is equipped with a checker or bottle top for a shooter.

Players.—From two to six may play at once.

Object.—The object is to advance the checker by snapping it

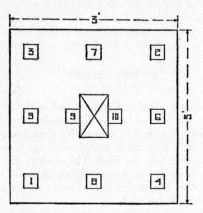

FIGURE 26

with the thumb and forefinger through the ten bases of the court in proper sequence.

The Play.—The players shoot in turns. Each starts by placing his checker at the spot marked X. He shoots for square Number 1. If he makes it he continues shooting for the other bases in sequence until he misses. He resumes playing next turn from the spot where the checker stops.

If a player strikes an opponent's checker in shooting he may have an additional turn and may also skip the next base for which he is due. After a player has made a successful shot he may remove his checker to a more advantageous spot if he chooses, provided the checker is not removed from the base in which it rests.

If a checker goes out of bounds it is returned to the boundary line at the point where it went out, from which point it is played when the player has his next turn.

Misses.—The play is a miss (1) when a checker fails to come to rest within or touching the proper base; (2) when a checker is shot out of bounds; (3) when a checker comes to rest touching a diagonal line of the pit.

The Player Starts Over.—The player must start over by returning his checker to the starting point (1) if his checker goes out of bounds on two consecutive turns; (2) if his checker comes to rest in the open space of the pit or touching the boundary lines of the pit (if it touches the diagonal lines of the pit the shot is ruled only as a miss). If the checker rests on a dividing line between the pit and bases Number 9 and Number 10 it is ruled as being in the pit.

Scoring.—The player wins who is the first to complete the round of the bases and reach Number 10.

London

Home, Sidewalk, Playground   *Children*

On a sidewalk or other smooth surface draw with chalk the court illustrated in Figure 27. Establish a throwing line six feet

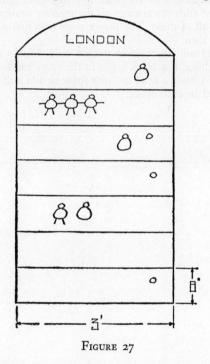

FIGURE 27

from the bottom end. Each player holds a disk or any small block of wood.

The first player slides his block into the court and, in the space in which it stops, draws a small circle representing a person's head.

The other players then throw in turn, putting heads in the spaces where their blocks come to rest. Several players may thus have heads in the same space.

The second time a player's block rests in a space in which he has already drawn a head, he draws a larger circle adjacent to the head to represent the body. The third time, he adds one leg and the fourth time the other leg. However, if the block comes to rest in a space where the player has not yet drawn a head, he draws one. Thus a player may have a number of partially completed men in the various spaces. As soon as a player has a man completed, he attempts to start a second man beside the first.

When a player has three men in a space complete except for the arms, he attempts to slide his block into this space again and when he succeeds he adds the arms to all the men by drawing a straight line through all of them. The player wins who first puts the arms on the three men.

Players may add to their own men only. Blocks resting on a line score nothing. If a block lands in the space marked "London" the player may draw a head in every space or add a mark to a man he has started in each space.

CHAPTER IX

JOKE STUNTS AND TRICK GAMES

Skeegee Weegee

Party, Club   *Juniors to Adults*

BOYS and girls, or men and women, should be seated alternately in a circle. The leader explains the game, saying that
it is a sort of "follow the leader" type of game, and that
each in turn should do just as he does. The leader, sitting in the
circle, then reaches over and pinches the right cheek of the person
to his left, and says "Skeegee Weegee." This procedure is followed
by all around the circle.

The leader then says the same thing and pinches the opposite
cheek. In successive turns he pinches the chin, forehead, and finally
the nose. During all this time the victim is being beautifully
decorated by the person next to him, whose fingers are smeared
with lamp black or burnt cork.

The leader then produces a mirror, looks at himself in it, and
says, "Skeegee Weegee." The mirror is thus passed around the
circle until the chagrined victim sees his changed countenance.

PINCHY WINCHY.—This is exactly the same as the above game
except that as each player pinches the next, he says "Pinchy
Winchy."

Helping the Brother Out

Club, Party   *Intermediates to Adults*

This is an excellent trick for an initiation especially in a secret
or semisecret organization which deals in passwords and signs.
In parties when used as a forfeit, the victim may be told that he is
to be initiated into the Loyal Lodge of Loons and then proceed
with the trick.

The victim is seated in a prominent chair to the front. When the
time arrives a dignitary of the fraternity says "The brother will
please stand and state the thirteenth password." Not knowing it,
he becomes embarrassed and says that he can't say it. The leader
then talks privately to him on the side:

Leader: "You mean to say that you don't know the thirteenth
password?"

Victim: "No."

Leader: "You should—it's been told to you. I think the best way out of the situation will be for you to make a clean breast of it and tell the brothers that you don't know the password, and ask if there is a brother present who will help you out. Say it just that way."

The victim then arises and says to the lodge:

"I'm sorry, but I don't know the password. Is there a brother present who will help me out?"

Whereupon three or four of the strongest brothers shout "Sure" and leap to their feet, grab the victim and help him out and off the porch.

The Court of the Shanghai Empress

Club, Party　　　　　　　　　　　　　　*Intermediates to Adults*

The ones to be the victims of the joke or initiation are asked to leave the room. The others seat themselves in a semicircle facing the Empress who occupies her throne. The Empress doubles her left leg under her and sits on it, and in its place hangs a carefully stuffed stocking which is put inside her slipper so as to make it resemble her real leg.

The first victim is called in and the leader explains with much "business": "In the court of the Shanghai Empress there is a peculiar ancient custom that all who enter must shake well the left leg of every person in the court, reserving until the last the extending of this honor to the Empress."

The victim begins the shaking and gets along quite well until he attempts to shake the left leg of the Empress and is startled when that member comes off.

Brother, Behold the Sacred Sign

Fraternity, Club, Party　　　　　　　　　　　*Intermediates, Seniors*

This stunt works best as an initiation trick in a club or fraternity. Precede the trick with solemn ceremony or a serious talk to the brothers on the sacredness of the secret sign. Then lead the one to be initiated or the victim of the trick to the front and stand him with his back to the group. The initiator stands facing him. Both the initiator and the victim hold a saucer containing some trivial token supposed to have a secret meaning in the fraternity. The bottom of the victim's saucer is blackened with lamp black or powdered charcoal.

The initiator, in the ritualistic fashion of initiations, and very impressively, states that he will now give the new brother the sacred sign. He tells the victim that he must pay the strictest of attention and repeat every movement of the sign exactly as he does. Furthermore he must look eye to eye at the initiator as the sign is conveyed.

The leader then touches the token in the saucer, rubs his finger in the bottom of the saucer, and draws various symbols with his finger on his forehead, cheeks and chin. The victim, following every move, does likewise.

Then the initiator announces to the group that he desires to present the new brother, who turns to face the group with face decorated fantastically in black.

Initiation to the Iowa Fraternity

Club, Fraternity, Party   *Juniors to Adults*

Three confederates are in on this joke. Put three chairs in a row. Bring in the person to be initiated and seat him in the center chair with a confederate on either side of him. The third confederate acts as High Priest. He solemnly asks one of the confederates to take three steps before him, then three steps backward, bowing each step and imitating a barnyard animal which the High Priest names (a cow by mooing, a pig by grunting, etc.). After the three steps backward he turns toward his chair and bows to it before sitting down. After the first confederate has done this most solemnly, the second confederate goes through the same ritual with the leader designating a different animal. Then the one being initiated is asked to do the same, imitating the cackle of a hen. While he is bowing to the High Priest and cackling like a hen, one of the seated confederates slips an egg on his chair. The candidate does not see the egg until he turns and bows to his chair. This finishes his initiation with laughter.

Ten-Cent Fortunes

Parties   *Juniors to Adults*

Three sit down solemnly beside a table containing a glass of water to have their fortunes told. The victim is in the center, and the three join hands to establish the psychic chain. It is explained that each is to be permitted to ask two questions answerable by a number. The victim might ask, "How many thousand will I be making a year when I am thirty-five?"

A dime is dipped solemnly in the glass of water and pressed against his forehead—it will stay there. He is then told to shake his head and the number of shakes required to dislodge the dime will be the answer to his question. He shakes—three, four, five, six—he will be making six thousand dollars!

Now for the second question: "How many children will I have when I am thirty-five?" Once more the dime is dipped and pressed firmly against his forehead, but this time it is removed—the water and the pressure produce a sensation causing him to think it is still there.

He begins to shake—five, ten, fifteen, twenty violent shakes and still there is no end.

Barnyard Music

Parties   *Juniors to Adults*

This starts out as a noisy stunt but soon turns into a joke on one of the members. The leader gives each guest the name of a barnyard animal to imitate, being careful to assign to the victim the task of braying like a donkey. At the signal each shouts his call—one barks like a dog, another whinnies like a horse, a third crows like a rooster, and so forth. All goes well the first time, and then the leader quiets everyone down to give the signal to start again and asks all to start their call quickly and loudly when he waves his hand. The signal is given and not a sound is heard except from the victim, who sounds forth loudly with a donkey solo. All the others, of course, are "in the know."

Zig-Zag Walk

Party, Club   *Juniors to Adults*

Place several objects of varying sizes at irregular intervals across the floor—milk bottle, pan of water, pile of books, gold-fish bowl, large mirror, and sheet of fly paper. Have the victim walk over them, carefully judging the location and height of each, and the distance between them. Then blindfold him and tell him to walk back over the course.

While he is being blindfolded, remove all the objects from the floor. The victim then high-steps and straddles his way carefully across the vacant floor. Instructions from the side lines help to steer him and congratulate him on his success.

The I Know Club

Party, Club   *Juniors to Adults*

The leader announces that all who are not already members may now join the I Know Club, provided they possess certain information. Everyone must be informed about some subject to be admitted.

The leader says "I know law, so I am admitted. What do you know, Mr. Bitters?" If Mr. Bitters says that he knows some subject which contains the letter "i," he is refused admission. Mr. Bitters says "I know politics," to which the leader replies "That's too bad, you can't join! Please stand over here in the blackballed section." Miss Selters, who sits next in line, says "I know music," to which the leader is forced to reply "That is most unfortunate, Miss Selters, your application to the I Know Club is refused." She also joins the blackballed section. Then Mr. Rickey says "I know tobacco." "That's excellent, Mr. Rickey. Congratulations. You are admitted," replies the leader.

So it goes until all have made their bid for membership. There will probably be many more refused than admitted. The leader then explains the secret of eligibility to the unfortunate ones and says that perhaps the decision may be reconsidered if they all kneel reverently in Chinese fashion and utter the Chinese Prayer, explained below.

The Chinese Prayer

Party, Club   *Juniors to Adults*

This is a hoax and should be used on a few whom for some reason the group wishes to submit to a joke. The leader asks all to kneel on both knees and place their foreheads on the floor. When all are in position the leader asks them to repeat after him, line by line, the Chinese Prayer:

> I know my heart,
> I know my mind,
> I know that I'm
> Stuck up behind.

Egg Balancer

Party, Club   *Juniors to Adults*

The leader places a carton containing a dozen eggs on the table and claims that he can balance an egg on a lead pencil. He attempts and fails, and the egg smashes on the table. The leader says that he can't work with so much noise and confusion, and asks all to be very still. He attempts to balance a second egg and it too breaks, making the table very messy.

The leader then becomes temperamental and upbraids the group for their lack of cooperation and courtesy in not keeping quiet. When his third attempt fails and the egg breaks, he loses his temper, picks up the remaining eggs and throws them at the crowd.

The guests scream and scatter before they discover that the eggs being thrown are rubber eggs. The success of this stunt depends on the effect produced by breaking the eggs on the table.

Rubber eggs may be purchased at a theatrical supply or novelty store.

Holding the Bucket

Party, Home, Club   *Intermediates to Adults*

Fill a heavy tumbler or small kitchen bowl with water, stand on a chair, and place it against the ceiling; then place a stick under it with which to hold it, and remove the chair. Challenge the un-suspecting one to hold the stick and dance a jig, or hold out his hand and kick it, or some other very simple stunt. This he does easily, but when he completes it he finds himself deserted by the guests and holding the glass against the ceiling with no way to get it down. Try this on a man—ladies do not take kindly to water spilled on their party dresses.

The stick should be just long enough so that the glass can be reached with it by holding the arm overhead.

When conditions permit, a large bucket of water may be placed on the ceiling.

The Royal Order of Siam

Party, Club   *Juniors to Adults*

Like the Chinese Prayer this is a joke on the performers and should be played with a few participating and the majority watch-ing. The leader asks the players to kneel, bend forward, and stretch their arms out, placing the palms on the floor. The first move is to learn the salute—from the above position, slowly rise until the arms are extended overhead, then slowly bend to the floor again. Next the accompanying words are to be learned. To the first time the arms are raised, say "Oh wha," the next time say "Tagoo," and the last time "Siam." Repeat over and over, increasing the speed gradually until they realize that they are saying:

> Oh, what a goose I am
> Oh, what a goose I am, etc.

Tumbler Tumbling

Party, Home, Club   *Intermediates to Adults*

Ask the unsuspecting one to hold out both hands, fingers ex-tended, palms down. Place two full glasses of water on his fingers, one on the fingers of each hand. He is then asked to repeat such a little rhyme as "Mary Had a Little Lamb." This, of course, he does successfully, but finds that no one offers to remove the glasses, and he is confronted with the dilemma of getting rid of them.

Lighthouse

Parties *Intermediates to Adults*

The most distinguished gentleman present is selected as the lighthouse. He stands up in the middle of the room and radiates that precious gleam of light from his eyes. Now the leader asks for several rocks to surround the lighthouse, kneeling on the floor and facing it. A buoy or two and a couple of boats are then stationed near by, all kneeling.

The biggest and huskiest have been saved for the waves. When the scene is all set the leader says, "The waves will now pound and beat upon the rocks!"

Animal Candy Scramble

Party, Club *Juniors to Adults*

This is a joke event based on Candy Scramble. Arrange the players in a circle and place a piece of wrapped candy in the center. Tell the players that you are going to whisper a name of an animal to each, and when the name of an animal is called, those holding that name are to rush for the candy and the one who gets it may have it. Caution them not to tell others their name because it will affect their chances. Then whisper the name of the animal to each.

The leader starts by telling the story of the circus menagerie, while all the players remain on their toes and ready to dash for the candy. When he mentions "Monkey" everyone in the circle dives for the candy.

Who Hit Me?

Party, Club *Juniors to Adults*

This is a joke stunt of ancient vintage, but it invariably works, nevertheless. Two players, one wise and the other the innocent victim, lie on the floor and spread a blanket over themselves. The wise one should see that their heads are well covered and that the blanket is tucked down between their heads so that they cannot see each other.

The rest of the group stand close around the blanket. One, a confederate of the wise one, holds a cane. The leader explains to the two under the blanket that one of the group will hit them with the cane, and if they can pick out the guilty person he will have to exchange places with the one hit. When all is ready, the wise one under the blanket reaches out with an arm and his confederate hands him the cane. He hits himself with it, tosses it on the floor, yells "Ouch" and sits up, pointing to someone as the person who hit him. They then lie down again and the wise one cracks the innocent one; both sit up and pick the one who they think did it. This goes on and on, the wise one cracking the victim harder and harder, until at last what is happening suddenly dawns on him.

The wise one can help the stunt along by talking to the victim under the blanket, complaining about how hard they are hitting, and asking the group to hit more gently.

Who Is It?

Party   *Juniors to Adults*

The victim is sent out of the room. The players, sitting in a circle, call the victim in and tell him that they have a person in the circle in mind, and he (the victim) is expected to find out who it is by asking questions of the players which they will answer with "Yes," "No," or "I don't know." The victim is not permitted to ask two consecutive questions of the same player.

Each player except the victim understands that the person selected is the one sitting to his right; that is, no one person has been selected, but many.

The victim may ask a player "Is it a boy?" and if the player's righthand neighbor is a boy he answers "Yes." The victim then asks another player "Does 'it' sit near you?" and the answer is "Yes." He then asks questions of others which would identify all the boys sitting near that player but none of them seem to be "it." The victim soon becomes hopelessly confused. This is a great fun-maker to all but the victim.

Squeak Baby

Parties   *Intermediates to Adults*

The guests are standing about the floor in close proximity to each other. One player (the victim) is selected to serve as "it." The leader announces that there is a squeak baby in the crowd and that "it" must find it in the hands of someone. When it is found, the player holding it becomes "it." While the leader is talking, someone pins the rubber squeak baby to the coat tail of the victim and then everything is ready.

When the victim's back is turned, someone presses the squeak baby and makes it squeak. The victim keeps whirling around until he guesses that it is on his back or is told.

WHO HAS THE WHISTLE?—This is played exactly like the above except that a whistle is attached to the victim's back. A very small and light whistle must be used.

The Endless Raveling

Parties   *Intermediates to Adults*

Place a spool of thread in a coat pocket and run one end through the coat so that it hangs out two or three inches. Someone will certainly be kind enough to remove the raveling and to his surprise find that it seems to have no end.

Boots without Shoes

Parties   *Juniors to Adults*

The leader instructs the players to say words as he directs. He then approaches one and says "Boots without shoes." The player responds by saying "Boots without shoes" but is informed that this is not correct. He then repeats the statement to the next player with the same remark. He continues until someone discovers that "Boots" is the answer expected.

Jumping over the Haystack

Parties   *Juniors to Adults*

A stack of chairs and other furniture is piled up in the center of the room to a considerable height. The leader says to the one to be initiated, "Do you see these chairs arranged in this pile? Take off your shoes and jump over them!" The innocent one surveys the pile and insists that it can't be done. The catch is that the player is supposed to jump over his shoes.

Whom You Love the Best

Parties   *Juniors to Adults*

While the victim is out of the room, the queen takes her place on the throne. The victim is caused to kneel before her. The queen commands "Say whom you love the best!" After the victim makes some sort of admission of love, the queen informs him that this is not adequate, and repeats her command. This continues until the victim stumbles on the fact that he is merely expected to say the words "whom you love the best."

Newspaper Touch

Parties   *Juniors to Adults*

Two players are given a newspaper and instructed to stand on it so that they cannot touch each other. The two try all possible positions only to find that they can always touch each other. The trick is to spread the newspaper in a doorway and close the door, one player remaining on each side of the door.

Leg and Arm Circles

Party, Home *Juniors to Adults*

Stand on the left foot and swing the right leg in a large circle from left to right. There is nothing difficult about this and it goes nicely. Then with the right hand, describe a large number "6" and continue the leg movement.

The movement "6" isn't even necessary—just try to swing the right arm in a large circle in the opposite direction from that used by the leg.

Crossed Fingers

Party, Home *Juniors to Adults*

Have someone extend the arms at full length in front. Tell him to cross the hands, palms together and fingers interlocked, then from this position bring the hands toward the chest and turn them upward. Now point to one of his fingers and tell him to wiggle it, or raise it, quickly.

He will have trouble doing this and will persist in wiggling the equivalent finger of the other hand. The finger must not be touched, however, or it can be easily moved.

Poke Your Head

Party, Home *Juniors to Adults*

Give the victim a key ring and tell him to poke his head through it. Insist that it can be done. If he fails to catch on, demonstrate for him: Stick your finger through the ring and poke your head.

KEYHOLE.—Say to the victim: "I can put myself through a keyhole, can you?" If he fails to get the idea, show him how by writing "myself" on a slip of paper and shoving it through the keyhole.

Eighth Wonder of the World

Party, Home *Juniors to Adults*

State that you will show the folks something they have never seen before and will never see again. Then crack a nut and hold up the kernel and ask if anyone has ever seen this before. Then eat the kernel and ask them if they will ever see it again.

Only One Word

Party, Home *Intermediates to Adults*

Give the victim the following list of letters and tell him to arrange them in only one word: D, W, N, O, E, O, N, R, O, Y, L. After some study he will probably give up. The trick is to arrange the letters to spell "Only one word."

Blindman's Lunch

Parties *Juniors to Adults*

Two players only participate in this event, but it is much enjoyed by the spectators. Blindfold the two and seat them on the floor just within arm's reach of each other. Give each two crackers. They attempt to feed each other.

Drawing the Moon

Parties *Juniors to Adults*

The leader announces that he will outline the full moon on the floor and put in the eyes, nose, and mouth. He asks each to do exactly as he does and outline a moon also. The trick is that the leader draws the moon with his left hand. Very few will detect this.

THE MOON IS ROUND.—The leader asks the players to do and say as he does and says. He then circles his face with his index finger saying, "The moon is round." He then points to his eyes, nose and mouth and says, "The moon has two eyes, a nose, and mouth." The players attempt to duplicate the movements and expressions, but for some reason cannot get them right. The trick is that the leader uses his left hand.

Strong Man

Party, Club *Juniors to Adults*

A person boasts that any five of the strongest men in the group cannot prevent him from drinking a glass of water. The person takes the glass of water in his left hand, and holds the arm out straight while the strong men all grasp the arm with both hands. When all is ready, he suddenly reaches out and takes the water in his right hand and drinks it.

Six Legs

Parties *Juniors to Adults*

Ask a person to leave the room with two legs, and come back with six. If he thinks quickly enough, he will leave and come back carrying a chair.

Egg in the Tumbler

Parties *Juniors to Adults*

Place a tumbler near the edge of a table. On it place a pie pan, and put an egg in the pie pan so that it rests directly over the top of the tumbler. With everything arranged, ask the guests to drop the egg into the tumbler, without touching the egg, the pie pan, or the tumbler.

If no one figures it out, demonstrate how it is done. In making the arrangements, you were careful to see that the tumbler was placed over a leg of the table and that the pie pan extends beyond the edge of the table an inch or two. Now hold a house broom beside the table leg, place your foot against it and push against the leg, pull the handle back and let it go so that it will spring back and hit the edge of the pie pan. The pan will go sailing across the room, and the egg will be reposing in the tumbler.

CHAPTER X

FORFEITS FOR SOCIAL GATHERINGS

ANY games and contests call for paying forfeits, that is, the loser is asked to perform some stunt. In social play, as a rule, the forfeit should not be paid at the time the player commits the act demanding a forfeit—that often interferes with the game being played. The procedure usually is to ask the player to turn over to the leader some small object from his pockets which the leader holds until late in the evening when the forfeit stunts are performed and the articles returned to the owners.

The time-honored method of conducting the forfeits is to appoint a judge and have him sit on a chair with a list of forfeit stunts in his hand. The leader stands behind the judge and holds one of the forfeit articles over his head where he cannot see it, saying

"Heavy, heavy, hangs over your head."

"Fine or superfine?" asks the judge.

"Superfine" says the leader if the article belongs to a girl; "Fine" if it belongs to a boy.

The judge then pronounces the penalty which must be performed by the player.

The following forfeits are suggested:

SING A LULLABY.—Hold a sofa pillow and sing a lullaby to it, gently placing it on the floor.

MOVING LUNCH.—Tie an apple or doughnut to a string and suspend it from the ceiling. Eat the doughnut or apple.

MILK BOTTLE STOOL.—Sit on an inverted milk bottle, hold feet off the floor, and sing or whistle a tune.

JUMP THE BOTTLE.—Set a milk bottle on the floor. Hold one foot up behind, grasp it with the hand, and jump over the bottle.

PICK UP PAPER.—Set a newspaper on end on the floor. Hold one foot up behind, hold it with one hand, bend over, and pick up the paper with the teeth.

HAND ON ELBOW.—Place one hand where the other can't reach it. (Place it on the elbow.)

COMPLIMENT YOURSELF.—Say five complimentary things about yourself.

CHINESE GET UP.—Hold the arms and lie on the floor. Get up without using hands or elbows.

AFFIRMATIVE ANSWER.—Ask a question that cannot be answered negatively. (What does YES spell?)

STIFF-KNEE PICK UP.—Stand with back against the wall, stoop and pick up a piece of paper off the floor without bending the knees.

IMPROMPTU ACTING.—Imitate one of the following:

> Rip Van Winkle waking up.
> A typical typist.
> A classical pianist.
> A farmer on Broadway.
> A soap box orator.
> A country boy proposing.

SALESMEN.—Make a sales talk for cornplaster.

KNEE BEND.—Raise one leg behind and hold it up with one hand. Lower the body until the knee of the raised leg touches the floor. Then stand erect again. The free hand may help balance but must not touch the floor.

TELLING THE TRUTH.—Answer truthfully four questions asked by anyone in the group.

MAKING RHYMES.—The player is asked to state two words that rhyme. After he has done this, he is told to make a poem using them.

ORATORY.—Make a one-minute speech on cheese, matrimony, censorship of the movies, or some subject appropriate for the group.

COMPLIMENTS.—Pay a compliment to five different people in the group.

STIFF-ARM TRANSFER.—Ask the person to stretch his arms out sidewise parallel with the floor and make them rigid. Place a book in one of his hands, and then tell him to transfer it to the other hand without bending his arms either at the elbow or shoulders. This is accomplished by laying the book down and then picking it up with the other hand.

ADMIRATION.—Give five reasons why the ladies (men) admire you.

PROPOSAL.—Demonstrate how you would propose to a lady (man).

CLICK HEELS.—Stand with heels about a foot apart. Jump upward and click the heels together twice and land feet apart as before.

JUMP THE LINE.—Draw a line on the floor and stand with toes touching it. Bend down and grasp the front of the toes with the hands. Jump over the line without losing hold of the toes.

LIFT THE CHAIR.—Kneel on the right knee behind a light straight-back chair. Take hold of one of the back legs of the chair with one hand and lift it from the floor. This is not so much a test of strength as of knowing how.

KNEE BALANCE.—Kneel on both knees and fold arms behind the back. Place a handkerchief in wigwam fashion on the floor about eighteen inches in front. Bend over and pick up the handkerchief with the lips without losing balance. The handkerchief must be placed just the right distance in front, depending on the size of the individual—too close and it is no stunt at all, too far and it cannot be done.

HAWK DIVE.—Place a handkerchief on the floor and kneel on the right knee about six inches from the handkerchief. Raise the left leg behind and grasp it with the left hand, using the right hand for balance. Bend down and pick up the handkerchief with the mouth. No part of the body but the right leg may touch the floor.

WHITE VOLCANO.—A coin is placed in the bottom of a pan of flour. By blowing the flour, the player tries to locate the coin and secure it with his lips.

HEAD PIVOT.—Draw a line two feet from the wall. Toe this line facing the wall, place the top of the head against the wall and fold the arms behind the back. Using the head as a pivot, circle the body around and back to the original position without crossing the line or removing the head from the wall.

BALANCE SQUAT.—Stand at attention, place the hands behind the back, and grasp the left wrist with the right hand. Squat and touch the floor with the finger tips without separating the heels. The heels may be raised from the floor.

CHAIR BEND.—Place a handkerchief on the floor eighteen inches in front of a straight-back chair. Sit on the chair facing backward. Fold the arms and clasp the legs around the legs of the chair. Bend over backward, pick up the handkerchief with the mouth, and come up to a sitting position again. The chair should be steadied by someone.

TIGHT-WIRE WALKING.—Stretch a string across the floor and give the performer a pair of opera glasses. Looking through the glasses the wrong way, he attempts to walk the full length of the string, placing his feet on the string as though he were walking a tight wire. A sensation of being high in the air is produced, and the results are amusing.

DIME ON NOSE.—Ask the player to lie flat on his back on the

floor and place a dime on his nose so that it rests perfectly horizontally. Tell him to wiggle his nose and put the dime off. He can't do it.

DIME-DIZZY.—Have the victim hold a dime in his fingers directly over the top of his head. Then spin him around ten or twelve times, tell him to drop the dime and pick it up. Be ready to catch him if he makes a head dive at the piano.

YAWN.—Yawn and keep on yawning until someone else in the group yawns.

OTHER FORFEITS.—The following events, described under other headings in these pages, are excellent forfeits. The reader will be able to adapt them to the forfeit scheme with very little thought:

Holding the Bucket.	Drawing the Moon.
Tumbler Tumbling.	Crossed Wires.
Who Hit Me?	Pat and Rub.
The I Know Club.	Coin Snap.
Chinese Prayer.	Cork Snap.
Royal Order of Siam.	Hitting the Penny.
Boots without Shoes.	Helping the Brother Out.
Jumping over the Haystack.	The Court of the Shanghai Empress.
Newspaper Touch.	Brother, Behold the Sacred Sign.
Poke Your Head.	Leg and Arm Circles.
Only One Word.	Crossed Fingers.
Whom You Love the Best.	Six Legs.
Blindman's Lunch.	

INDEX